BENETTON FORD

A Racing Partnership

BENETTON FORD

A Racing Partnership

PHIL DRACKETT

The Crowood Press

First published in 1990 by
The Crowood Press Ltd
Gipsy Lane, Swindon
Wiltshire SN2 6DQ

British Library Cataloguing in Publication Data

Drackett, Phil, *1922–*
    Benetton Ford : a racing partnership.
    1. Formula 1 racing cars. Racing
    I. Title
    796.72

ISBN 1 85223 374 5

Typeset by Inforum Typesetting, Portsmouth
Printed and bound in Great Britain by BPCC Hazell Books Ltd, Aylesbury

Contents

	Foreword	7
	Acknowledgements	9
	Preface: Wheels of Fortune	11
CHAPTER 1	Prelude to the 1990s	15
CHAPTER 2	Birth of a Team	31
CHAPTER 3	'United Colors of Benetton'	53
CHAPTER 4	Nuts and Bolts	63
CHAPTER 5	The Drivers: Travelling in Hope	91
CHAPTER 6	The Drivers: 'The Four Horsemen'	102
CHAPTER 7	The Drivers: The Benetton Boys	107
CHAPTER 8	The Drivers: Men of Tomorrow?	113
CHAPTER 9	AD 2000	129
CHAPTER 10	Old Soldiers Never Die	180
	Appendix: How They Fared	183
	Index	191

Foreword

Running a Formula 1 team was never one of the initial goals of the Benetton family. As Phil Drackett so clearly illustrates in his book, Benetton grew quickly into their ownership. As Benetton stores sprang up around the globe it became evident we needed a productive advertising and promotional medium.

Therefore, the choice to enter the Formula 1 arena was quite simple. From a global marketing standpoint, Formula 1 is the most cost-effective way to reach an upscale worldwide audience. The Formula 1 World Championship offers extensive media coverage, television broadcasts to all major countries and large spectator attendance at each venue. Equally important to Benetton S.p.A. is the opportunity to meet with our representatives and licensees to discuss the intricacies of their markets.

Our partnership with Ford started in 1987 and has expanded each year. In 1990 we began a commercial relationship with Ford where Benetton Formula employees coordinate Ford's worldwide Formula 1 marketing activities.

I believe you will enjoy *Benetton Ford: A Racing Partnership* because it fully explains the foundation that will bring Benetton Formula great successes in the 1990s.

Alessandro Benetton,
President, Benetton Formula Ltd.

7

Acknowledgements

'I know what you writer fellers are like,' said Gordon Message, Team Manager of Benetton Formula 1 – and it didn't sound too much like a compliment. Which makes me all the more grateful to Gordon and the Benetton Ford team for their readiness to help with this book.

Director Flavio Briatore, jetting around the world in the interests of his company, has sometimes been an elusive man to track down but when we have spoken his co-operation has been extended without restriction or hindrance. In his absences, his staff have always been most helpful. I am especially grateful to Steve Madincea whose liaison work between Benetton, Ford and the author has been prompt, friendly and efficient.

It was extremely kind of Alessandro Benetton, present President of Benetton Formula Limited, to agree to write a Foreword. In a few words he has managed to encompass the underlying theme which runs throughout the book and he has my most sincere thanks. Not all of today's tycoons are so forthcoming.

The Ford Motor Company have also been extremely helpful – but then they always are. My special thanks to Michael Kranefuss, a major figure in the Benetton Ford story, and to my old friends, Harry Calton and Stuart Turner for help, suggestions and encouragement.

Assistance has also been forthcoming from former Benetton team manager, Peter Collins; Barry Griffin, of Goodyear Tyres Racing Division; John R Creak, of Mobil Oil; Jardine PR, consultants to Camel and Team Lotus; and Grand Prix Racewear, of London.

In a pause for breath between commentaries, a few words of encouragement from Murray Walker convinced me that we were right to believe that there are people who would like to read about the partnership between Benetton and Ford, a marriage yet to make the headlines.

My thanks to Arthur Barker Ltd for permission to use an extract from my book, *Brabham: Story of a Racing Team*; and to *Rabbit*, magazine of the United Benetton Supporters' Club. Not for the first time I have poached a story from my longtime pal, Eoin Young. One of these days he'll send me a bill.

Photographs are an important part of most books and I have endeavoured to include some pictures which, whilst not of Toleman, Benetton or Ford personnel and equipment, help to convey the atmosphere of the periods involved.

I am very grateful to Steve 'On-the-ball' Clark, Head of Ford's Photographic Unit, and that super-efficient Antipodean partnership of Nigel Snowdon and Diana Burnett, who between them provided a significant number of the illustrations, both in colour and black-and-white.

The imaginative Zooom photographic team, headed by battle-hardened motor racing expert John Dunbar came up with the fine jacket illustrations and some others besides. Gerry Stream, whose picture of a rabbit being chased by a racing car at Brands Hatch is still talked about, delved deep into his files to produce some fine coverage of the Toleman era.

More pictures came from Colin Taylor, Archie Knowles, P J McDonagh, the RAC, Motor Circuit Developments, Marlborough, Avenue Communications, Rank Films, Eurosport TV, Denim, VAG (UK), Camel Team Lotus, JPS, Team Lotus, Benetton, Lola and Renault.

Michael Cooper and Geoff Goddard gave valuable time to digging into their photo files and Paul Damen, in whom the milk of kindness flows, was the only lensman prepared to risk his equipment by photographing the author.

Any bleary 'Box Brownie' shots which have crept past the editor's eagle eye are the woeful work of the author.

Last, but most certainly not least, my thanks to Neal Eason-Gibson, historian, book collector and RAC motor sport executive, who, not for the first time, has provided the statistical rails upon which to run my train.

To anyone left out, my apologies and the promise of a pint of real ale when next you visit that fine city of Norwich or one of its motoring outposts, the race circuit at Snetterton or the headquarters of Team Lotus at Ketteringham.

Phil Drackett
Mundesley-on-Sea
Norfolk
June, 1990

Preface: Wheels of Fortune

The partnership of Benetton and Ford came about almost by accident. From 1967 through to 1983 the Ford-Cosworth DFV 'normally-aspirated' engine had dominated Grand Prix racing but, with the assurance of the governing body that such engines would be excluded at the beginning of 1986 and that turbocharged engines would form the basis of Formula 1 for several years to come, Ford decided on a purpose-built 1½-litre turbocharged V6 engine, again in partnership with Cosworth, to be ready for the 1986 season.

Hollywood star Paul Newman as he appeared in the film Winning. *In real life Newman is a capable race driver and co-owner of the Haas team which played an unwitting role in the Ford and Benetton partnership.*

Alan Jones testing the Beatrice Grand Prix car. It was certainly an impressive car to look at but one season's racing was hardly enough to show if the car had real merit.

Britain's Eric Broadley, head of Lola Cars, who was design consultant on the Beatrice-Lola-Ford project and has been the man behind many outstanding cars.

Alan Jones, of Australia, 1980 World Champion Racing Driver, who came back to drive for the Beatrice-Lola-Ford team of Carl Haas. Patrick Tambay, of France, was the other driver.

Some teams had had the experience of as much as nine years developing turbocharged power and it was obvious that, to catch up, Ford would have to do some of their own testing and development work in actual races. This meant either starting a new team and doubling the headaches or finding a ready-made team prepared to go into partnership on the venture.

Cometh the hour, cometh the team. During the previous year an American, Carl Haas, had entered the Grand Prix scene. He was the co-owner with film star Paul Newman of an Indianapolis team for which Mario Andretti was No. 1 driver and which was sponsored by the giant Beatrice conglomerate which included Samsonite, Avis and STP amongst its subsidiaries.

The new Beatrice-Lola car was engineered and operated by Formula One Race Car Engineering (FORCE), a British-based company run by two former directors of the McLaren team, Teddy Mayer and Tyler Alexander. Design consultant was Lola chief, Eric Broadley, who had provided the Newman-Haas team with its successful Indy car. The Beatrice-Lola was initially powered with a Brian Hart turbo and was driven by the Australian 1980 World Champion, Alan Jones, who came out of retirement to do so.

The pedigree seemed right. The set-up seemed right. Ford and Haas forged a new relationship and despite inevitable teething problems, the new Ford turbo engine acquitted itself not at all badly and solid progress was made. Jones had been joined by the French driver, Patrick Tambay, and between them they scored a modest six Championship points, four to Jones, two to Tambay, and the team was equal seventh in the Constructors' Championship.

However, for 1987, Haas decided to confine his activities to within the domestic American scene and Ford were left with the new engine and no car to put it in. Not for long. Benetton, following the company's buy-out of the Toleman team, had become one of the most promising as well as colourful Grand Prix teams and an agreement was reached with them. Substantial advances were made with the engine during the season and were reflected in the team's results. By the end of the season, the Ford turbo's race power output matched that of all rivals — a notable achievement by a late starter after just two seasons, one with Beatrice, one with Benetton.

The Benetton Ford relationship proved a continuing one. Yet it might never have happened had a certain Mr Carl Haas decided to stay in Grand Prix racing.

CHAPTER 1

Prelude to the 1990s

The red–and–white car was hurtling towards the chicane and a corner where the driver would have to brake down to something like 40mph – this was the slowest part of the circuit. Another red–and–white car was closing in on the first and, as the corner loomed up, the driver tried to dive inside the leader. As he attempted to do so the leading car turned in towards the apex of the bend, the two cars collided and slid together across the track like great slugs locked in an oily embrace.

The first driver got out and walked away, his face impassive, although some claimed to have seen an enigmatic smile. The second driver frantically urged the marshals to get his car back in the race, was push–started and kept going (with interruptions) to the chequered flag.

Then he was disqualified by the stewards.

Nannini was declared the winner of the 1989 Japanese Grand Prix when Senna was disqualified after his collision with Alain Prost.

The first driver was a World Champion, the diminutive Frenchman, Alain Prost. The second was also a World Champion, the Brazilian, Ayrton Senna. Their duel for the 1989 World Drivers' Championship overshadowed everything else and was conducted in an atmosphere of bitterness and acrimony – so much so that, had the rivalry been in soccer, some of the principals would undoubtedly have been charged with 'bringing the game into disrepute'. The World Championship was 'indelibly tarnished' said one commentator as wars of words flooded the media and spilt over on to the Grand Prix circuits. The irony of it all was that the two main protagonists, Prost and Senna, were teammates, both driving for McLaren.

Their 'coming together' occurred in the Japanese Grand Prix, the fifteenth and penultimate round of the 1989 Championship. After Senna's

disqualification the race was awarded to Alessandro Nannini, No. 1 driver for the Benetton Ford team, his first victory in Grand Prix racing, albeit by default. And in the turbulence caused by the Prost–Senna vendetta, no one seemed to notice that Benetton Ford had had quite an eventful year of their own.

The backdrop to this extraordinary season was the exclusion of turbo engines from Formula 1 and a return to normally-aspirated engines. If most people in the game were honest they were also hoping for an end to the McLaren domination of the sport which, well-earned though it was, was in danger of bringing an air of boredom and disillusionment to a public tired of seeing the red-and-white McLarens first and second in nearly every race.

Turbo or not, there was no guarantee that McLaren would not continue to dominate.

Nannini on the victory podium in Japan, flanked by Riccardo Patrese and Thierry Boutsen.

They had the pedigree – 70 victories, 6 Drivers' Championships and 4 Constructors' Championships. They had the engine – the Honda V10 and an exclusive agreement with the Japanese firm; and they had the two top drivers, the reigning champion, Senna, and the runner-up, Prost, winner of more Grands Prix than any other man.

Although there were more teams than ever bidding for places on the grid, Ferrari looked to be the only real danger with a car designed by the Briton, John Barnard, and an Anglo–Austrian driving combination of Nigel Mansell and Gerhard Berger.

A lot of hopes were realised when Mansell won the first race of the season, the Brazilian Grand Prix – but it was back to Senna first, Prost second, in the next race at Imola. Berger crashed in flames and it says something for the construction of the modern racing car that he was not severely injured although bits of his machine were flying all over the place.

It was during this San Marino race that signs emerged that all was not well between the two McLaren drivers with Prost allegedly annoyed at a 'breach of etiquette' by Senna. It was an atmosphere which carried over into the Monaco event but not to the extent of preventing another Senna–Prost triumph.

Prost could only manage fifth in Mexico where Senna won again and began to look like a 'shoe in' for the championship. However, typical of the ups and downs of the sport, Senna failed to finish at Phoenix, Arizona, and Prost took the winner's laurels.

The McLarens both failed to finish in the Canadian Grand Prix but it was the Williams team, not the Ferraris, who stepped in for a 1–2. Senna retired again in the French Grand Prix but Prost, who announced his intention of leaving the McLaren team at the end of the season, was the winner and the title race looked wide open again. By now Prost was making no secret of relations between himself and his team-mate; commenting on Senna getting away from the line first, although the Frenchman was in pole

position, Prost said, 'He must have jumped the start.'

At Silverstone, Senna slid off and Prost won again, but in Germany Prost lost the lead when his car jumped out of top gear and Senna passed him for another McLaren 1–2.

Britain's Nigel Mansell drove a fantastic race to win in Hungary with Senna second and Prost fourth but in the rain of Spa it was back to the old status quo: Senna first, Prost second and Mansell third. A McLaren driver seemed certain to win the World Championship. But which one?

And so to Italy.

Prost was complaining that his car was not as good as Senna's. The team-mates were not speaking to each other and the world's press was literally enjoying a Roman holiday. Ironically the Italian Grand Prix went to Prost and his 'not so good' car, Senna's engine failing.

The Portuguese Grand Prix brought about the biggest furore yet with Mansell's Ferrari team-mate, Berger, and Alain Prost making hay while Senna and Mansell feuded. Mansell was black-flagged after reversing in the pitlane but continued to race. Senna was lying second when Mansell tried to overtake him. The Brazilian moved across, the cars collided and both men were out of the race. There were bitter scenes afterwards with Mansell hauled up before the stewards, FISA's head man refusing to hand the trophy to Berger and the Ferrari and McLaren team managers exchanging benedictions upon one another's houses. The bottom line read that Senna's championship chances had virtually gone – he would have to win two of the remaining three races to take the title *providing Prost was unplaced*.

In Spain Senna won the first of the three but Prost was third. Senna *had* to win in Japan and Australia.

So came the hiatus in Japan with Senna and Prost destroying one another, Prost to retire, Senna to be disqualified. In the entire history of motor racing have team-mates ever combined before to ruin their own chances? And has a team

Nannini in the rain-swept 1989 Australian Grand Prix in which he finished second.

ever protested a decision which gave the World Championship to one of their own drivers as McLaren did on this occasion?

Fittingly, the stormiest-ever Grand Prix season ended in a rainstorm in 'sunny' Australia. Prost, the championship assured, retired after one lap when the race was started for the first time. Allegedly, most of the drivers agreed not to race unless conditions improved but under pressure they nearly all did. Some commentators said it illustrated the power that television has over sport today. In this case the worldwide TV satellite hook-up allegedly did not permit of undue delay so, rain or no rain, the race went on. Sixteen drivers went out in the blinding rain after the race started for the second time, and one of them was Senna who in almost nil visibility ran into the back of Martin Brundle's Brabham, an event graphically captured by the TV camera on Brundle's car.

Was it safe to race or not? Did the almighty dollar play a major role in influencing the decision? Or did the organizers genuinely believe that all was well? The Clerk of the Course was the former racing driver, Australia's Tim Schenken, who presumably would have some sympathy for his fellow drivers after five years in Grand Prix himself. Later, the Confederation of Australian Motor Sport was to issue a statement denying that commercial pressure influenced the decision to run the race in any way whatsoever. Senna's abrupt exit meant that the winner's laurels were left to Thierry Boutsen and the Williams team.

If God was on Senna's side, as some folk said the Brazilian believed, then He deserted him in the driving rain of Adelaide. Senna went home to Brazil to think things over. Prost, with his third

Thierry Boutsen in his Williams on the way to victory in the Australian Grand Prix.

Martin Brundle, 1988 World Sports Car Champion and Ford Segrave Trophy winner, was shunted up the rear by Ayrton Senna in the 1989 Australian Grand Prix. If it wasn't for the smile on his face it might look as if he was going after Senna with a gun.

Nannini passes J J Lehto's abandoned Onyx during the 1989 Australian Grand Prix.

19

world title and a 1990 contract with Ferrari in his pocket, presumably consoled himself with the thought that there had been a happy ending after all.

The Senna–Prost–Mansell shenanigans overshadowed what was happening among the lesser lights, not least one of the most promising of the 'minnows', the Benetton Ford team. Their year was an eventful one (although if acrimony accompanied any of the ups and downs at least it was in private and not public chatter) for Benetton ended the season with a different team manager to the one with which they started, a double change of drivers, a new engine and a new Head of Development. That, plus a first Grand Prix win for a long, long time made it quite a busy year . . .

The night soil only hit the fan once . . .

Benetton Ford started the season with Alessandro (Sandro for short) Nannini as No. 1 driver and Englishman Johnny Herbert in the No. 2 seat. The latter's potential was generally regarded highly but a horrific crash at Brands Hatch the previous August had resulted in such bad injuries that many of the pit road experts considered Team Manager Peter Collins was taking a big risk in giving Herbert a drive.

After the first six races of 1989, Herbert was replaced in the team by Honda McLaren test driver Emmanuele Pirro. The official statements were bland. Herbert: 'In the interest of my long-term future and ultimate recovery.' Collins: 'We have no intention of releasing him – we are convinced of his long-term potential.'

Space man: Sandro Nannini kitted up for action.

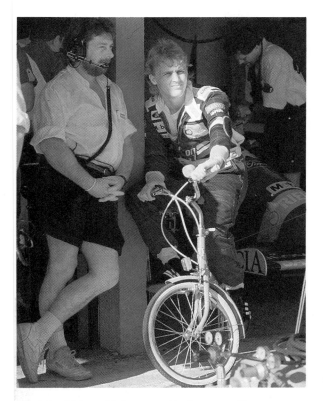

The injured Johnny Herbert uses a bicycle to get to his car during the 1989 Brazilian Grand Prix.

Emmanuele Pirro: the man without helmet.

Chorus: 'But he must have a rest from the pressures of Grand Prix racing.'

Which shows that press releases are rarely worth the paper they are duplicated on. By the time of the Spa Grand Prix Mr Herbert was presumably rested – because he was behind the wheel of a Grand Prix car again. Only this time it was a Tyrrell.

Some thought the Benetton Ford team's administrator, Flavio Briatore, a Benetton executive, was behind Herbert's departure because he wanted another Italian driver in the team. Others claimed that Michael Kranefuss, head of Ford Special Vehicle Operations, was the man behind the change, Ford having a powerful voice in the project.

Those who held to the latter theory also voiced the opinion that Kranefuss was trying to

induce British designer, John Barnard, to leave his post as Technical Director of Ferrari and join Benetton. Whatever Kranefuss did or did not have to do with it Barnard did sign a contract with Benetton and left Ferrari at the end of the season. Which tended to strengthen the theory that Kranefuss was also behind the Herbert move.

Whatever the rights and wrongs of the Herbert affair Peter Collins soon followed him, to be replaced by Gordon Message who had been with the Witney-based team since it began life as Toleman.

Pirro saw out the season (the cynics observing that he failed to get as many points in ten races as Herbert had done in six – and, most of the time, Pirro had a better car and engine) but had to make way in 1990 for the three-times

Gordon Message, Benetton team manager (left) with one of his drivers, Emmanuele Pirro, during the 1989 season. Pirro replaced Johnny Herbert in the team.

World Champion, Nelson Piquet, a refugee from the disappointing Lotus team which was but a shadow of the great teams of Colin Chapman's heyday.

Benetton began the 1989 season with updated versions of the old B188 cars equipped with Ford DFR engines but later in the year they were expecting to have designer Rory Byrne's B189 and a new, lighter, Ford engine.

In the run-up to the first Championship race of the season in Brazil, the team undertook a test programme with three cars, during which they covered something like 1,800 miles (2,896km). Two of the cars had normal suspen-

sion, the third was fitted with an active suspension system on which the team was carrying out development work. This third car was in the hands of Johnny Dumfries, otherwise the Earl of Dumfries and heir to the Marquis of Bute. The other two cars were driven by the 'works' drivers, Sandro Nannini and Johnny Herbert.

The heat was stifling and remained so up to the race. A great deal of attention was focused on Herbert and there was much speculation on how the newcomer would fare, especially since he appeared to be suffering in the heat. Some people said he had to be carried to his car which was something of an exaggeration – he used a

The Benetton Ford B188. This was the car with which Benetton started the 1989 Grand Prix season.

bicycle although, like every other Grand Prix driver, he had to be assisted into the narrow confines of his cockpit and strapped in by other hands.

East Londoners are made of stern stuff. Behind the wheel Johnny showed little sign of injury or distress. He drove brilliantly in this, his first Grand Prix, and showed his team-mate Nannini the way to go, eventually finishing fourth, just 10.5 seconds behind the winner. It was a good start to the season for Benetton Ford since Nannini held firmly on to sixth place and another scoring point.

The new B189 was tested before the San Marino Grand Prix but was not thought ready to run in the race. Despite this Nannini finished third. Herbert worked hard but a spin set him back in the pecking order and in the end he did well to finish eleventh.

With third, fourth, sixth and eleventh as the harvest from two races, the outlook for Benetton looked promising.

There had been hopes that the new car and the new Ford Cosworth V8 engine would be ready for the Mexican Grand Prix but all thoughts of this had to go when the engine developed a crankshaft problem. Peter Collins admitted to disappointment. He said:

23

The Benetton Ford 189, the new car introduced midway through the 1989 season which would win a World Championship race.

'Nannini tested the car at Paul Ricard and put in some good times. The durability of the crankshaft is the problem and it is an un-expected one since the engine has done a lot of running on the dynamometer without any ill-effects but, of course, there's always an element of doubt in any engine that you can't determine until you get it into the car.

'We will obviously have to continue with the old car until Cosworth Engineering and Ford have sorted the engine out. I'm still convinced that ultimately it will be a very good car but meanwhile we are not going to be as competitive as we would have liked. But we'll give it our best shot.'

The faster circuits best suited the Benettons so it was no surprise when they drew a blank at Monaco (eighth and fourteenth); but, on the quicker Mexican circuit, Nannini was fourth and Benetton Ford had moved up to second in the Constructors' Championship, McLaren (who else?) being in front. Herbert finished fifteenth.

The US Grand Prix was held at Phoenix amidst the dry heat of the 'High Chaparral' country. It looked good for the team when Nannini qualified third fastest but he crashed on the 'warm-up' lap of all things and had to start the race in the spare car. However, the crash had caused damage to his neck muscles and back

– he spun twice and he was forced to give it best on lap 10.

Herbert was nearly equal to the challenge. Despite the stifling heat, the pain in his right foot, a locking front brake and losing fourth gear long before the end, he brought his car home in fifth place, a meritorious performance after working his way from the back of the field. The frequent brake applications demanded by the street circuit were just what a driver already suffering a right foot injury needed . . .

'Débâcle' was the only word to describe the happenings at the Canadian Grand Prix. Rain fell steadily and when Berger stalled on the grid, the start was abandoned and the field set off again in formation. At this point Nannini and Nigel Mansell both had the same idea. Believing that the weather was going to improve they went into the pits to change to dry tyres under the impression that the race was now under way. The race had *not* started and both were disqualified.

Their protests that there was no red light at the end of the pitlane – undeniable – were overruled, once more giving rise to the belief that there is one law for competitors and another for officials. It was the last straw for the Benetton team as Johnny Herbert had failed to qualify.

It was after this that Herbert 'withdrew' from the team 'following discussions between Benetton Ford, Herbert and his medical advisers.' Pirro took his place in the French Grand Prix and finished ninth. Sandro had the new car, complete with new engine, and hopes were high in the Benetton pit when he was in second place at the half-way mark but a good drive ended when the left rear suspension failed. Herbert was there in spirit – all the team wore 'Johnny Herbert' badges on their overalls!

The French race was no flash in the pan. When the circus moved to Silverstone for the British Grand Prix, Nannini not only finished third but also set the third fastest lap.

In Germany the team had three of the new cars and Nannini was the fastest man on the circuit until forced out by a faulty ignition sensor when he was lying fifth. Pirro too was going great guns despite a 'coming together' with Thierry Boutsen which ended with the Belgian's Williams collecting the wall, prompting the gentleman in question to make enquiries as to Mr Pirro's parentage.

Pirro had moved up to fourth place, when, on lap 27, he lost it and crashed at high speed through some of the big polystyrene blocks being used as barriers. Fortunately his injuries were not serious, one leg being gashed and the other badly bruised. Despite the calamities it looked very much as if the new cars would give Benetton that little extra required to make the team truly competitive.

It did not happen in Hungary although Pirro placed eighth after Nannini's gear selectors retired him with 46 laps gone but on the rain-sodden circuit at Spa it looked as if things were beginning to come together for Benetton, Nannini winning a private battle with Derek Warwick (Arrows-Ford) to hold on to fifth place with Pirro placed tenth of sixteen finishers. It was a creditable performance, especially by Sandro, since the Benetton was not reckoned the easiest car to handle in the wet and the Italian was constantly harassed by Warwick.

Rail-bird cynics were a little more intrigued by the fact that the 'unfit' Herbert reappeared in this race driving one of the Tyrrells, but they were robbed of any duels in the damp between Johnny and his former team-mates by the over-eagerness of the Essex driver which led him to spin off on his third lap, first retirement of the race.

There was more drama offstage. Just two days before the race it was announced that the Benetton Ford Team Manager, Peter Collins, had resigned and his assistant, Gordon Message, had been promoted in his place. For the 35-year-old Gordon it was a reward for loyal service since he had been with the team and its predecessor Toleman from the beginning, having started in motor-racing as a mechanic with March.

25

Nigel Mansell (seen here in his John Player Special days) drove a fantastic race to win the 1989 Hungarian Grand Prix for Ferrari.

The official announcement gave no reasons for Collins's departure, leaving people to draw their own conclusions, but it did clearly specify the divisions of power within the team set-up. Message was responsible for 'the direction, policy and operation of the team's entries in the World Formula 1 Championship'. Chief Designer Rory Byrne, another stalwart, was responsible for 'design and development of the Benetton Ford B189 Formula 1 car'. Flavio Briatore, 'previously working with Benetton's clothing operations in North America and Europe', would be responsible for 'the direction and administration of the team's commercial activities'.

London-born Message is unmarried and has devoted his life to motor-racing, a decade at Witney, Oxfordshire, having been preceded by his spell with the March team. He was – and is –

Peter Collins, the man who picked Herbert as a future star.

a man with the belief that the essential ingredient in motor-racing is *consistent* competitiveness, something which, as he laughingly remarks, is, 'Easy to say or write but – unfortunately – very difficult to achieve.'

Into his shoes as Chief Mechanic came Nigel Stepney.

The Italian Grand Prix, which came next on the championship schedule, was one for the new 'think tank' to forget. Pirro (gearbox trouble) failed to complete one lap and although Sandro was up with the front runners for a long time he eventually retired after 33 laps with brake trouble.

Fortunately, or unfortunately, depending upon your point of view, the McLaren 'Civil War' then at its height, almost completely engaged the attention of the press who were far too busy to bother about the shortcomings, alleged or real, of any other team. Even the Italian journalists, who usually had an extra turn of the screw for anyone with Italian connections, could not find time to hold a post-mortem on Benetton's lapses. Not even the announcement, six days prior to Monza, that the 37-year-old Brazilian and three times World Champion, Nelson Piquet, was leaving Lotus to join Benetton in 1990, created too many headlines. There were more than a few people prepared to say that Piquet was over the hill, although in fact the third of his world titles had been as recently as 1987. The driver himself and his new team manager admitted to no such doubts. Gordon said:

'I'm delighted. We believe he is still one of the quickest drivers contesting the World Championship but, in addition to that, the experience he has gained in winning three titles will be invaluable to us in testing and development work. With his aid we will be able to delve more deeply into a number of concepts and ideas, some of them quite revolutionary, which are now under consideration.'

Piquet himself made no secret of the fact that the continued support of Benetton by the Ford Motor Company and exclusive use of the new Ford Formula 1 engine influenced his decision. 'It can be a race-winning combination,' said he, 'I'd be very happy if we could beat Ferrari and finish the championship second or third.'

Piquet had his first run in a Benetton Ford B189 on a murky November morning at Silverstone. After a morning at the wheel Piquet was even happier about events, declaring that the Ford power plant outstripped the Judd used by Lotus and he could see it beating Ferrari and Williams-Renault in 1990 although he still thought it would be hard to beat Honda (McLaren).

Simultaneously with the news of Piquet's signing, Benetton said they would keep Johnny Herbert under contract although Sandro Nannini would partner Piquet in World Championship races. Herbert would test drive for the team in 1990 and, hopefully, graduate to the Formula 1 team in 1991. Meanwhile, to extend his Grand Prix experience, negotiations were in hand for him to drive with other teams in 1990. Pirro, meanwhile, would be released from his contract at the end of the 1989 season.

And *that* season was by no means over for the team from Witney. In the stormy and controversial (both on and off the track) Portuguese Grand Prix, Nannini finished a very creditable fourth, despite a spin, to Berger, Prost and Johansson. Pirro retired after 29 laps.

In Spain, Nannini spun again and this time there was no going on; then the unfortunate Pirro was forced out after 59 laps with cramp. Pirro is a fairly tall man and the close confines of the Benetton cockpit were too much for him on this occasion. Driver accommodation in the racing cars of the 1980s and 1990s may be safer than of yore but is not too high in the comfort stakes. The American driver Eddie Cheever, a big fellow, literally had to be forced into his Arrows-Ford during the 1989 season – which may perhaps have influenced his decision to switch to sports cars! Certainly some great drivers of the past, Mike Hawthorn for instance,

As the 1980s dawned, the following drivers who would play a role in the Toleman/Benetton story were listed by the *FIA Year Book* as considered among the more successful non-graded drivers: Rad Dougall, Teo Fabi, Brian Henton, Stefan Johansson, Nelson Piquet and Derek Warwick. They would shortly be joined by Thierry Boutsen, Eddie Cheever and Eddie Jordan (who became more famous as an entrant).

Others listed included Derek Bell, Alain Prost, Keke Rosberg, and Nigel Mansell. Didn't they do well? . .

would have great difficulty in the modern machine. The ideal build for a modern Grand Prix pilot would be similar to the physique of between-the-wars 'Bentley Boy', George Duller – and his 'daytime job' was that of jockey!

The penultimate round of the Championship was the Japanese Grand Prix where, of course, the Senna versus Prost affair finally came to a head.

Shortly after the two McLaren cars came together when Senna attempted to overtake Prost on the inside, the situation virtually repeated itself when Senna came up behind Nannini. Sandro obviously had not the slightest desire to be grasped in the warm embrace of the McLaren and gave the single-minded Brazilian a clear passage.

It was a decision which more than paid off because when Senna was disqualified it was the good-looking Italian who stepped on to the winner's rostrum and although Sandro confessed he would have been happier to have won without the involvement of the stewards, a win it was, a first for the driver and Ford's first Formula 1 victory since Michele Alboreto (Benetton-Tyrrell-Ford) won the Detroit Grand Prix in 1983.

Meanwhile, Pirro's ill-fortune continued, the No. 2 Benetton driver having an accident after 33 laps.

The team went on to Australia and the last round of the championship with another 'back-stage' appointment to think about: Ferrari's British designer, Technical Director John Barnard, was to take up a similar appointment with the Benetton Group. His main task would be to establish the Benetton Technical Centre, a new facility additional to the team's HQ at Witney. Flavio Briatore described it as a 'major step forward' in a reorganization which had begun earlier in the year with the appointment of Alessandro Benetton, son of Luciano, as President of Benetton Formula Limited.

How all the 1989 appointments would work together remained to be seen ('brilliant but abrasive' was one contemporary description of John Barnard) but for the moment the rainswept streets of 'sunny' Australia awaited the Grand Prix circus, not to mention more arguments and controversy. Despite everything, it was another good race for Benetton with Nannini second and Pirro (in the points for the first time) fifth. There were crashes galore in the appalling conditions and only eight cars finished. To finish was not only an achievement but also required a certain amount of luck.

A little piece of television history was made during this race. Martin Brundle's Brabham was fitted with a rearview TV camera and viewers all over the world were treated to the scary spectacle of Senna's McLaren looming up through the mist and the rain to smite poor Brundle up the back end.

It brought to an end a season which despite all the changes in team and administrative personnel had not been a bad one for Benetton Ford. Sandro Nannini had finished sixth in the World Drivers' Championship behind Prost, Senna, Patrese, Mansell and Boutsen and ahead of such luminaries as Berger (seventh) and Piquet (eighth). Johnny Herbert was fourteenth in the list and Emanuele Pirro twenty-third. It was Nannini's best year to date with one win, one second and a total of eight points finishes. More often than not he qualified amongst the ten fastest.

Benetton Ford finished fourth in the World Constructors' Championship which is just

Alain Prost in happier days — at a contract signing (left) — and winning the British Grand Prix for Renault (below).

about where anyone in motor-racing would place the team on the world scene. Despite the strife which rent the team, McLaren remained on top of the pile with Ferrari and Williams in hot pursuit.

Ferrari owed much to the technical genius of Barnard – and he would be with Benetton next season. Nannini was improving – and was to be joined for 1990 by the proven Piquet. It meant that Benetton would be one of the few teams with a starting line-up of two drivers who had won a Grand Prix (many, in the case of Piquet).

In recent years only McLaren, Ferrari and Williams had had the pleasure of such luxuries (if luxury it could be called in the cases of Prost and Senna). Most teams would have been grateful for just one winner in the line-up. The icing on the Benetton cake was that the new Ford engine was being sorted out.

It all looked very promising for a team which had its beginnings a decade earlier in a story which involved such diverse characters as a British road-haulage contractor and a Venezuelan motorbike rider . . .

CHAPTER 2

Birth of a Team

An Italian fashion house – and a British road-haulage contractor. There could hardly be a greater contrast yet, in a motor-racing sense, one gave birth to the other.

The Benetton Ford Grand Prix team of the late 1980s had two parents, one of which, the Italian, we shall come to later. The initial parental influence, however, came from the little town of Witney in Oxfordshire.

The successful Toleman Transport Group first became involved in motor-racing in the 1970s. Ted Toleman was (and is) a swashbuckling character with much more than an ounce of the daredevil in his make-up; so much so that, in addition to motor-racing, he has risked his neck in the Paris–Dakar Rally – regarded as akin to a suicide mission even by hardened competitors – and in the stormy waters of the Atlantic in trying

Ted Toleman left the Grand Prix circuits for the 'pleasures' of the Paris–Dakar Rally, the ultimate in mental, physical and mechanical endurance.

to break the record for the fastest crossing. As these words were written the bearded adventurer was planning another onslaught on the Atlantic, this time in partnership with the world landspeed record holder, Richard Noble, another whose life seems incomplete without the spirit of adventure.

The Toleman Transport Group first dabbled in motor-racing in humble club circles but became too enthusiastic to be content at that level and moved on to sponsoring in Formula Ford 2000 and then running a team in Formula 2. By 1979 plans were afoot for the Group to design and build its own cars. In 1980 Toleman dominated the European Formula 2 Championship with these cars powered by engines produced by Britain's Brian Hart and driven by two more Britons, doughty Midlander Brian Henton and 'yet to make a name' Derek Warwick. So successful were they that there was only one logical step for the Group to take – to move upwards into the very top echelon of Grand Prix racing.

That, of course, was a different story. To win Grand Prix races a team needs a very good chassis, an exceptionally good engine and at least one driver, or preferably two, capable of winning the Drivers' Championship – a recipe which is sometimes easier to find than the millions of pounds required today to finance such an operation.

Even successful businessmen like Toleman don't have bottomless purses (which is the ideal state for Grand Prix car owners). So it was a long and rocky road upon which the new Toleman Grand Prix team ventured for the first time in 1981. The team remained loyal to the people who had got them thus far: the Toleman

Swashbuckling Ted Toleman, founder of the Toleman motor racing team (far left) has since switched to powerboats and plans an Atlantic crossing with world land speed record holder, Richard Noble (second from left).

TG181 was powered by a Hart engine and the drivers were again Henton and Warwick.

That first season was a heartbreaker. From May to September the team religiously turned up for the Championship rounds – and went away again without turning a wheel in anger.

San Marino, Zolder, Monaco, Jarama (where they had the consolation of an additional sponsor, Diavia), Paul Ricard, Silverstone, Hockenheim, the Österreichring, Zandvoort . . . cars, drivers, transporter, mechanics . . . the wandering gypsies wound their way from one disappointment to another yet always setting off in hope for the next destination.

Finally, at Monza in the Italian Grand Prix on the 13th (of all days) of September, 1981, a Toleman made the starting grid. Better still, in the hands of Brian Henton, it finished. Even better still, it finished tenth but to the team it was almost as good as winning after so many heartaches and failures. It was also as good as a birthday present to Henton who would be 35 just six days later.

There was only a fortnight to the Canadian Grand Prix and reverting to failure but, in Las Vegas, Derek Warwick qualified one of the cars for the US Grand Prix. Unfortunately he did not finish, retiring on lap 43 with gearbox trouble

Silverstone and the British Grand Prix around the time Toleman switched from Formula 2 to bid for Grand Prix fame and fortune.

Derek Warwick who learned Grand Prix the hard way, trying to qualify Toleman against the world's best.

when in thirteenth place. However, it was another 'first' – Warwick's first Grand Prix race.

When a team is as far down the bottom of the mountain as Toleman was – two starts, one finish in twelve attempts, not to mention two car 'write-offs' (one at Dijon and one at Silverstone) – there is really only one way to go and that is upwards and that is the direction Toleman was to take. Mark you, the upward direction was at times so imperceptible that an outsider may have been forgiven for not noticing it.

The team started 1982 with cars that were variations on the 181, the 181B and the 181C, with engines from Hart. Derek Warwick was back in one car but Henton had gone and the vacant seat was taken over by an Italian, Teo Fabi. The 27-year-old from Milan had never driven Formula 1 but the previous season had been runner-up in the North American CANAM series, winning more races than any other driver.

33

The super-streamlined transporter especially designed for the Toleman team and a leader in its field.

Crowds at Silverstone by the bridge crossing the track. A shot taken in the early eighties when Toleman were newcomers on the Grand Prix scene.

There was also some sponsorship – from Candy, the Italian electrical appliances and machines manufacturer, long interested in motor-racing. There are sponsors and sponsors. Some will keep you going in cigarettes, some in beer, some in cameras and film. But Candy must be the only sponsor that keeps you clean. At one time Candy used to maintain washing centres in the pit area. At Silverstone one year they provided five washing machines and tumble driers in the paddock area and the service was available both to the racing teams and members of the public. Courtesy Candy and Persil.

No excuse for oily overalls.

The first three races of the season – South Africa, Brazil and the US – gave little indication of any great improvement over the previous season. The one glimmer of hope was given by Warwick in South Africa. Not only did he qualify for the race which, as we have seen, was by no means a certainty where Toleman was concerned, but he also covered 44 laps before being forced to retire after an accident. He was in nineteenth place at the time.

However, the first anniversary of Toleman's arrival on the Grand Prix scene was celebrated with both cars qualifying, something they hadn't done the previous year. Admittedly, Warwick retired on the first lap with electrical troubles and although Fabi finished he was 8 laps behind the leader at the chequered flag. And, to put the matter in perspective, one of modern motor-racing's many disputes was in progress at the time and a number of leading teams boycotted the race.

At Zolder for the Belgian Grand Prix, both drivers qualified but retired, Warwick when lying twelfth, Fabi seventeenth. Monaco, where both drivers failed to make the grid, and Detroit and Montreal, where the cars were withdrawn, were complete blanks but in the Dutch race, Warwick not only qualified in thirteenth position, the highest yet, but recorded fastest lap before retiring with engine trouble.

At Brands Hatch, Fabi was eliminated in a startline accident. Warwick stormed through to second place before retiring on lap 41, a very encouraging performance.

It was a sign of better times for the remainder of the season with two cars qualifying for most of the outstanding events and, in some cases, actually finishing; in itself, something for a struggling team to be pleased about.

Fabi did not qualify at Hockenheim and Las Vegas and retired in the French Grand Prix (lap 1), Austrian (lap 7), Swiss (lap 31, when lying twelfth) and Monza (lap 2). Derek Warwick did rather better, finishing tenth in Germany and fifteenth in France.

For the last two races of the season the team had the new car, the TG183. The designers, Rory Byrne and John Gentry, had been working frantically to get it into action and so get some practical experience before the season ended and 1983 dawned. Ironically, in his first time out in the new car at Monza, Warwick was sideswiped out of the race on the first lap when he was 'collected' by a spinning Tyrrell. Driver of the Tyrrell? Warwick's old team-mate, Brian Henton.

Cougar had part-sponsored the team in 1982 but for 1983 Candy were joined by Magirus, a company which made trucks and reminded one of Ettore Bugatti's acid comment many years before that Bentley were 'the fastest lorries in the world'.

The Tolemans, lorries or not (and it had to be faced that they were not exactly the loveliest cars on the circuit) were certainly faster than before. Improvements to the new chassis, close co-operation with the Pirelli tyre company and development of the Hart engine had all played their part and when the Grand Prix circus tested their machines at Rio in January, Warwick amazed many. The Ferrari team clocked him only fractionally slower than 'top dog' Alain Prost (Renault) while the Renault team made him faster than their own man. Either way it was an impressive performance which augured well for the future.

Warwick's team-mate now was another Italian, Bruno Giacomelli, an experienced man

Derek Warwick in the 1982 British Grand Prix. He drove well and was in second place when he was forced to retire on lap 41.

with fifty-six Grands Prix under his belt and a third place at Las Vegas in 1981 as his best showing. The partnership was to record more placings – and more scoring places – than Toleman had ever previously achieved. Moreover, only once (Giacomelli at Monaco) did one of the cars fail to make the grid. Giacomelli had a sixth (Grand Prix of Europe), seventh (Monza), eighth (Spa) and ninth (Detroit) to his credit. Warwick had his best season yet with two fourth places (Dutch and South African Grands Prix), fifth (Grand Prix of Europe), sixth (Monza), seventh (Spa) and eighth (Brazil).

In the majority of races where one or both

failed to finish the cars covered a goodly number of laps before retiring and several times retirement was nothing to do with car, engine or tyre failure. Bruno spun off at Rio and was involved in an accident in the Austrian Grand Prix. Warwick was twice involved in accidents, at Long Beach and at Monaco, where he was lying fourth after 50 laps when he had a 'coming together' with Marc Surer.

The landmarks were the team's first Championship points in the Dutch Grand Prix and both drivers in the points for the first time in the Grand Prix of Europe at Brands Hatch.

Giacomelli may recall the season better for

Monaco where Teo Fabi took a Benetton into eighth place in the Grand Prix of 1987.

Derek Warwick cornering in the 1983 British Grand Prix. Turbo problems forced him to retire on lap 27.

Bruno Giacomelli leading a Renault during the 1983 British Grand Prix.

another reason. After retiring in the Canadian Grand Prix in Montreal he was given a lift to the pits on the back of Keke Rosberg's car. He fell off and was badly bruised, dislocating three toes into the bargain.

Despite a comparatively successful 1983 season (or, in at least one case, perhaps because of it) there were considerable changes in the set-up for 1984. Sponsorship remained a problem (Iveco had replaced Magirus as co-sponsors late the previous year) and there were dramatic personnel changes.

The major change was the No. 1 driver. Warwick had been 'scouted' by several teams, Lotus and Renault among them, who had been impressed by his attitude, his determination and, of course, his driving skill. The English driver was most reluctant to quit Toleman, the team which had given him his big chance, and

One-time team manager at Witney, Peter Gethin, as a driver, was involved in Grand Prix's closest finish. At the wheel of a BRM, Peter won the 1971 Italian Grand Prix from Ronnie Peterson's March-Ford by 0.01 seconds. François Cevert's Tyrrell-Ford was third, 0.08 seconds behind Peterson and Mike Hailwood's Surtees-Ford a further 0.09 seconds away, fourth. As New Zealander Howden Ganley in the other BRM was only 0.43 behind Hailwood it meant that a miniscule 0.61 seconds covered the first five finishers. You can't get much closer than that.

where he had been most happy. Indeed, almost everyone associated with the team in those days is insistent that it was a happy team and that was the ingredient mainly responsible for such modest successes as they had.

However, some of the other teams offered

Ayrton Senna on his way to third place in the 1984 British Grand Prix – a promise of what was to come from the brilliant Brazilian.

The United Colors of Benetton appear in the 1985 British Grand Prix; the driver is Teo Fabi.

not only much more money but also, and in this case a major consideration to an ambitious driver, a real chance at Championship laurels. Reluctantly, he bade farewell to Toleman and signed with Renault. The French team had apparently been torn between Warwick and de Cesaris but decided the Englishman was the safer bet.

The new Toleman duo were the 24-year-old Brazilian, Ayrton Senna, tipped for a bright future by most of the experts, and 28-year-old Venezuelan Johnny Cecotto, who had forsaken two wheels for four. The team manager was Peter Gethin, son of a famous racehorse jockey and trainer, who had his own special niche in

motor-racing history. Peter startled the Grand Prix world when, driving for BRM, he scored a surprise victory in the 1971 Italian Grand Prix at a record speed of 150.75mph (242.55kph), which was to remain the fastest ever Grand Prix winning speed for many years.

Senna, too, showed that for once the experts were right. He was second in Monaco, where he also recorded fastest lap; third at Brands Hatch and Estoril; sixth in South Africa; and seventh in Belgium and Montreal. Warwick, it had to be admitted, was hardly missed.

There were just two blots on the landscape. Cecotto was badly injured in practice at Brands Hatch in July and took no further part in the

Monaco, the world's most glamorous circuit. The race circuit runs around the harbour . . .

. . . but if you live in the right place you get a very good perch . . .

. . . gendarme's eye view of the racers . . .

. . . but young lovers at a roadside bistro are oblivious to the roar of Formula 1 engines in the next street.

Championship being flown to Munich for treatment to both legs. And Senna, following an internal dispute, was suspended by Toleman for one race and did not take part in the Italian Grand Prix.

On the other hand, the 28-year-old London-based Swede, Stefan Johansson, Cecotto's replacement, drove well to finish fourth in Italy and eleventh in the final Grand Prix of the season in Portugal. Senna finished ninth in the World Drivers' Championship and might conceivably have been higher had he raced at Monza.

It was a great pity that, after doing so well in 1984, the next season was to be the team's last under the Toleman banner. They had a new car, the TG185, Teo Fabi was back in the driving seat with a new partner, Piercarlo Ghinzani; and there seemed little reason why they should not do well.

In the sequel it was a disaster over which it is best to draw a veil. The team missed the first three races of the year and failed to finish in any of those in which they took part save the Italian Grand Prix at Monza where Teo Fabi managed to finish twelfth. Benetton moved in, took over the Witney works and unveiled the Benetton-BMW B186, for the 1986 season. Fabi was retained as No. 1 driver and was joined by rising star Gerhard Berger.

The new set-up was almost an instant success, with Berger doing particularly well. He was sixth in Brazil and Spain, third in the San Marino, tenth at Spa, tenth again at Hockenheim, seventh in Austria, fifth at Monza and crowned it all with victory in the Mexican Grand Prix, a magnificent achievement and one which caused great delight in the Benetton camp. Moreover he was well-placed at the time in nearly every race in which he was forced to retire.

Fabi was not completely eclipsed by the talented Austrian. His highest place was fifth in Spain but he was seventh at Spa, eighth in Portugal and tenth in Brazil and Australia, giving Benetton a total of thirteen finishes, their worst patch coming in mid-season when blanks were registered in the Canadian, American, French and British Grands Prix.

The 1987 season saw Benetton with a new car, the B187, and a new engine, the Ford-Cosworth turbo. Teo Fabi was still there with '19' on his car but the new occupant of number '20' was the Belgian driver, Thierry Boutsen, who had been 3½ years with the Arrows team. He might well have taken over where Berger left off had not the team suffered from almost inevitable teething problems with the new turbo engine. In the opener at Rio, Boutsen was fifth, Fabi retiring with turbo troubles. At Imola they both retired well on into the race and when both were very well placed. Spa provided a similar story but Fabi was eighth in Monaco and, after both retired in Detroit, he finished fifth at Paul Ricard. At Silverstone, the two Benettons came home sixth and seventh, Fabi leading the way and, following a blank day at Hockenheim, Boutsen was fourth in the Hungarian Grand Prix.

Then came a purple patch. In Austria Fabi was third, Boutsen fourth; at Monza, Boutsen fifth, Fabi seventh; and in the Portuguese race, Fabi fourth and Boutsen fourteenth. Spain was a blank and then Fabi was fifth in Mexico. It was Boutsen's turn to be fifth in Japan and he climaxed a decent season for the team with a splendid third place in the Australian Grand Prix at Adelaide.

It looked very much as if the Ford turbo engine would soon score its first Grand Prix win, maybe to set off on a record run like that of the earlier normally-aspirated engine. Certainly hopes were high both at Ford and at Benetton. Fabi and Boutsen had both been on the rostrum, albeit in third place, and had finished ninth and eighth in the Drivers' Championship and the Benetton-Ford turbo team had been fifth in the Constructors' Championship. In motor-racing don't count your chickens . . .

Not for the first time, the sport's rulers had a change of heart. Ford had embarked upon a turbo programme on being assured that turbos would provide the motive power in Grand Prix racing for years to come. The writing was already on the wall for the turbos. Normally-aspirated engines, this time of 3.5-litre capacity, which had been readmitted to Formula 1 in 1987, would be the only permitted power form from 1989 onwards.

Ford were not 'best pleased', as they say in the Lotus county of Norfolk. Ford and Cosworth had fought hard during the formative years of the turbo era to protect the position of the normally-aspirated engine which, as they pointed out, was the type of engine around which Formula 1 regulations had been framed. They had gone into Formula 1 turbos simply because they were told that the turbo was going to be *the* Grand Prix engine. Now, suddenly, turbos were out and normals were in again.

Ford were certainly not against the principle of settling for one type of engine or the other in Grand Prix racing, simply because it was impossible to completely close the power gap between the two types. However, the unexpected change back to normal meant an end to the turbo development programme and left Benetton Ford with a problem for the 1988 season when either turbos or normals could be used.

Since the turbo had shown great promise in 1987 it was a temptation to use it again in 1988 in the hope that further improvement would lead to Championship victories. To do this would jeopardize the design and development programme of the new normal engine so the decision was taken, however, reluctantly, to

When Ford powers most of the cars at Brands Hatch why not have a Ford-powered pace car as well?

Bruce McLaren (left, top)*, Graham Hill* (above) *and Jack Brabham* (left, bottom) *were the inspiration for Peter Collins to try his luck on the motor racing scene in Europe.*

Peter Collins learned from a master, Colin Chapman (holding headphones). With Colin is another Aussie, the one and only Jack Brabham. The driver is the Italian-American, Mario Andretti.

send the turbos into early retirement. A further development of the Ford DFZ engine was on the drawing board, the Ford DFR, and for 1988 Benetton was entrusted with the exclusive use and further development of this interim engine which, from the begining of 1989, would replace the DFZ as Ford's 'customer' Formula 1 engine.

Some sort of moral justice prevailed because Benetton Ford *did* have a better season in 1988, turbo engines or no. At least one car finished in every race and more often both cars were highly placed. Boutsen was back with the team but another Italian, Alessandro Nannini, took over the seat previously occupied by Teo Fabi. The new boy had two third places, a fourth, a fifth, two sixths, a seventh, a ninth and an eighteenth.

Boutsen set a remarkable record for consistency being third in no less than six races, followed by a fourth place, a fifth, two sixths, a seventh, two eighths and a ninth for a total of fourteen finishes in sixteen races, the two he failed to finish in being the French and British Grands Prix.

Although the two drivers had to sacrifice the points they had earned in the Belgian Grand Prix for being placed third and fourth – there was an irregularity concerning the fuel specification – Boutsen was fourth in the Drivers' Championship and Nannini joint ninth.

McLaren-Honda had again won the World Drivers' Championship with its turbo-charged V6 engine but Benetton had easily defeated its non-turbo rivals and frequently had beaten many of its more powerful turbocharged opposition. Benetton were thus a clear third in the Constructors' Championship and first of the non-turbocharged teams.

And in 1989 Formula 1 would be for 3.5-litre normally aspirated engines . . .

One of the happiest men in the Benetton set-up was the Australian team manager, Peter Collins. Collins became a motor-racing enthusiast as a youngster 'Down Under', avidly watching the Tasman series in which top Grand Prix aces such as Jack Brabham, Bruce McLaren, Graham Hill, Jackie Stewart, Chris Amon and many others took part during the winter break from the World Championship series.

After leaving school Peter worked for a shipping company and an airline, jobs which bored him stiff but which in fact provided him with experience and knowledge which would be very useful to him later as a team manager. He decided to get into motor-racing full-time and felt his best chance would be in England. There is a story which may or may not be true to the effect that he spent most of his wedding night on the telephone long-distance trying to get hold of Colin Chapman to ask him for a job.

Be that as it may, Peter and Jane Collins landed in London in 1978 without jobs and with few prospects. It took nearly a year of trying before Peter finally landed the job he sought with Lotus.

The late Colin Chapman could be a hard taskmaster and did not suffer fools gladly but he buzzed and whirled with ideas, was full of energy and was certainly the right man for someone seeking knowledge of the racing game to listen to and learn from . . .

Collins worked for him for three years then went to the ATS team for a brief spell before joining Williams where he played an important part in organizing Keke Rosberg's World Championship year. Appropriately, the Finnish driver won the Detroit Grand Prix in 1985, the last race before Collins left the team.

Pete joined Benetton at Witney and was able to develop his particular talent for spotting drivers. Berger and Boutsen were two great signings although his signing of Johnny Herbert did, as was said earlier, arouse great controversy.

Collins was looking to the future and, encouraged by the outcome of the assistance Benetton had given to Johnny Herbert the previous season and which had helped to bring a promising new recruit into the Grand Prix fold, he decided to extend the idea.

He talked with the UK subsidiary of a Japanese telecommunications firm, Uniden, which had not previously been involved in

Peter Collins, who brought his bride from Australia, in a bid to break into a motor-racing career.

motor-racing and they were taken with the idea of encouraging young drivers. The outcome was the Uniden-Benetton Formula Driver Scholarship and the objective was to give a young driver of promise the opportunity to step up from Formula Ford to Formula 3. A scholarship place had been arranged for the recipient with West Surrey Racing, the team which had won the British Formula 3 Championship with Ayrton Senna and again with Jonathan Palmer,

47

Collins played a role in Keke Rosberg winning the World Championship.

both of whom had gone on to Grand Prix racing, although, of course, with greatly contrasting success.

Derek Higgins, from Slough, was chosen as the recipient of the 1989 Scholarship. At the start of the year the future looked bleak for 24-year-old Higgins. He had a burning ambition – to become a Grand Prix driver – and very little else. He had no sponsor and little hope of a Formula 3 drive. Then, after a series of test drives and interviews, the delighted Higgins was informed that he was the first recipient of the Uniden-Benetton Formula Driver Scholarship – a fully-paid drive for the season in the British Formula 3 Championship. He soon started to repay his benefactors with a win, a second place and a lap record. 'With everything else taken

care of, I can concentrate all my energy into driving well.'

The miracle could not have been achieved with just any driver of course – the pedigree had to be right. Higgins had won both Junior Formula Ford titles in 1987 and repeated the feat in the Senior category in 1988 – only the expected flood of offers from Formula 3 did not materialize. 'In February, Gordon Message phoned and in two weeks from his call I went from being an unemployed Formula Ford champion to having a drive with the top team in Formula 3 and a lifeline to one of the top Grand Prix teams.'

Only time will tell if Higgins has a future in Grand Prix racing during the last decade of the twentieth century. If he does, then a great deal will be owed Peter Collins who, when he left Benetton during the 1989 season, left a team in good shape and with great potential.

Toleman is now but a memory in so far as Grand Prix racing is concerned but years on many people still talk about the team with affection. 'They were such a happy crew,' said one. It was a team which inspired loyalty and Derek Warwick was evidence of that. 'They were my greatest friends,' he said.

Trailing the others or not the team always gave 100 per cent effort and Brian Henton was not one whit behind Warwick in this. Some pundits have wondered how Henton ever settled into the team. The answer was not hard to find. The man who was British Formula Vee champion in 1971 and British Formula 3 cham-

Bookselling race buff New Zealander Eoin Young tells a story about Lori Acquati, whose book and model shop stands in the middle of the Monza Grand Prix circuit. Acquati mentioned that one of his best customers is the former Benetton team manager, Peter Collins. 'He buys books and models – and anything to do with Peter Collins'. Said Young, 'But why would a cynical Aussie be interested in a 1950s Ferrari racer?' 'Why?', reiterated a slightly amazed Lori, 'Because that ees hees name too.' Ask a silly question . . .

Rosberg tries out his Williams on the modified Spa circuit in Belgium.

pion in 1974 had always fought hard; he earned the admiration of all those in the know in 1978 when he campaigned on a shoestring in Formula 2, driving a privately-entered March 782-Hart 420R in competition with some very well-financed teams. Bruno Giacomelli in a works March cleaned up the field but Henton put up some spirited performances and was fifth at the Nürburgring, eighth in Rome, fourteenth at Rouen, eleventh on his home circuit of Donington where he recorded the fastest lap in record time, 108.55mph (174.701kph), sixth in Sicily, eleventh at Misano. Though only sixteenth in the final Championship placings, Henton had certainly provided some excitement along the way.

When you realise that Henton did it with no main sponsors (and at the time they reckoned you needed £120,000 for a full Formula 2 season), the car was on the 'never-never' and he was singularly lacking in spare engines, you have to agree with the writer who said it was all down to '100 per cent effort plus Henton's belief in himself'. That effort, that belief, frequently put him near the front of the grid, produced some very fast lap times and from time to time had him out in front of the pack and setting a sizzling pace. In the four Championship races he was not a finisher, one was an accident, the other three electrical faults, battery lead and clutch trouble. If he and his team had not had to watch the pennies and could have splashed out more on engines and equipment it would not be unreasonable to hazard a guess that Henton

49

A South African driver was prominent in the early days of Toleman. Rad Dougall, born in Johannesburg on 7 September 1951, began racing at Kyalami in 1971 and threw up his job as a development engineer to come to Europe in 1975. He did well in Formula Ford in his first season in England but in 1976 crashed at Mallory Park and broke both ankles.

Recovering, he had his first Toleman-backed drive and in 1977, again backed by Toleman, he was outstanding in Formula Ford 2000, winning two championships.

When Toleman went into European Formula 2 racing in 1978 and 1979, Dougall went with them and put up some good performances including a win at Thruxton but, by 1980, Brian Henton and Derek Warwick were the Toleman 'works' drivers.

would have finished in the top half-dozen. Certainly his performances gained enough respect for him to be invited to join Rad Dougall in the Toleman team the following season.

Another character of those early Toleman days was not a team driver but an engine specialist. Brian Hart had been a driver, good enough and fast enough to break the Silverstone Short Circuit outright lap record with a speed of 89.61mph in a 1,498cc Lotus 20-Ford Cosworth. But that had been back in 1962 since when Brian had established a reputation as a top-rate engine man.

In that year of 1978, Formula 2 was dominated by March chassis, followed by Chevron. About two-thirds of the cars competing were powered by BMW engines. With the withdrawal of Renault, most of the others employed improved versions of the Hart 420R. In only three races were Hart-powered cars not on the front row of the grid and, four times, Hart-powered cars roared to victory. Bearing in mind the comparative resources of BMW and Hart, the latter employing about ten men at his Harlow headquarters in Essex, this was quite an achievement. The Hart engine was also somewhat cheaper than the BMW, about £7,500 a time compared with approximately £9,000. All the same, one can understand why Brian Hen-

ton, as a privateer, was inhibited from having spare engines hanging around the place. Moreover, the original cost of an engine was not the whole story. A rebuild was advised after 600 miles (965km) and the cost of that at the time was well over £1,000. And to get the picture in proper perspective you only have to think how much the cost of living has gone up during the past twelve years or so.

In some ways Brian Hart is a man in the Harry Weslake mould. That grand old man 'breathed on' Grand Prix engines, sports car engines, production car engines; on motorbike power plants for road-racing and on speedway bikes. The Weslake speedway unit wrested world domination from the Czech Jawa concern. Harry's method was to work on cylinder heads, pistons and the like to extract extra power. Brian did much the same thing and so a Hart engine, without being redesigned, would show continually improved performance over a longish period.

Hart worked well with the Toleman team and they went into Grand Prix racing still using Hart power and Hart turbo power, the best year being 1983 with five scoring finishes in Grand Prix races. When Benetton took over the team, there was one season with BMW before embarking upon the association with Ford.

Nevertheless, Brian Hart has a well-earned niche in the world of competitive motoring, an engineering genius fit to be mentioned in the same breath as Duckworth, Weslake, Railton, Judd and other Britons who have made Britain great wherever cars, boats and planes are raced. Warwick's verdict: 'I really rate the guy.'

The Irish Grand Prix driver, Derek Daly, who twice won Formula 2 Championship races in 1978, using a Hart engine, was another who thought highly of the man and his engine, rating the latter as better than its BMW rival. What is often overlooked is that, at the time, Formula 2 cars with the Hart Formula 2 engine were not doing badly in the Aurora AFX Formula 1 Championship, where much of the competition came from genuine Formula 1 cars.

Ski-jumper turned race driver, Divina Galicia, with her Ford turbo-powered sports car.

At Zandvoort, the Dutch driver, Boy Hayje, finished third on his home territory, driving a Chevron-Hart. Ahead of him were Bob Evans and Divina Galicia, both in Surtees-Fords. At the second Brands Hatch race, Elio de Angelis won in a Chevron-Hart, with the Americans, David Briggs and Don Breidenbach, also in Chevron-Harts, eighth and tenth. The New Zealand driver, Brett Riley, was fifth at Mallory with Iain McLaren tenth. At Daytona, the eldest of the Brabham boys, Geoff, finished sixth in a Box-Hart.

The strongest Hart representation of the Championship was at Thruxton where the Bri-tish driver, Geoff Lees, finished fifth, with Briedenbach sixth. Stephen South was ninth, Norman Dickson fourteenth and David Briggs seventeenth. Add in a ninth place for Carlo Giorgio, of Italy, in the first race at Brands and Harts did not do too badly up against McLaren, March, Surtees, Ensign, Wolf Williams and the like. These 'names' were mostly powered by Ford, although there was a sprinkling of BRM, BMW and so on.

Brian Hart's power units did even better in 1979 in Formula 2, thanks again largely to the input of Brian Henton. The Toleman team was going great guns and if only their new Ralt cars engines – insufficient intercooling and poor throttle response – but recognising and curing them were two different things.

Brian tried different water-to-air intercooling systems in the same race. One car had separate water-cooling, the other used a more conventional method employing the engine to cool the water. The turbo itself was switched to the top of the engine, the cooling area was increased and so on and so on. And all the time this was going on, Brian was also working on a revised specification monobloc engine.

Imagine the relief when at last a Toleman car not only qualified but actually finished.

Hosannas in Harlow . . .

Such joys are often short-lived. Just when Brian Hart thought he had everything sorted . . . Toleman had three or four of the new monobloc engines in hand for the start of the 1982 season. The engines were running well and giving no trouble. Their performance and reliability were improving all the time. Yet the cars were still not achieving. Why? Said Toleman spokesman and well-known motoring journalist, Chris Witty: 'We have chassis problems.'

Well, there's not much a poor old engine designer can do about that, so Brian had to let Rory Byrne and his design crew put that right and in due course they introduced a new chassis. Over at Harlow, they worked hard all the winter, improved the engines and devised an experimental electronic fuel injection system. Then the team ran into tyre trouble . . .

It turned out all right in the end however. The introduction of Holset turbochargers put the last part of the engine jigsaw in place and the team came up with its first Grand Prix points.

But if you think that was the end of the engine-builder's troubles then Brian Hart would probably be happy to disabuse you . . . always assuming that he can find an hour or two to spare . . .

Brian Hart's engines were prominent in the Toleman era and Elio de Angelis drove a Chevron-Hart to victory against Formula 1 machinery.

had been ready in time Hart could well have enjoyed more victories than ever. As it was Dougall had to start the season in his old March and, of course, when both team drivers had their new cars there was still a settling-in period.

Those Formula 2 years were just 'overture and beginners' for Brian Hart. When the Toleman team crossed over into Grand Prix racing in the turbo era, it brought a whole lot of headaches in its train. While the drivers battled on the track to qualify, Brian was battling just as hard behind the scenes to get the power units right. The main problems were not uncommon to turbocharged

CHAPTER 3

'United Colors of Benetton'

To the average member of the public, a sponsor is a shadowy figure or corporation prepared to pour thousands or, in the case of motor racing at least, millions into a sport primarily for the amount of television coverage to be gained. Easy, providing you have the money.

Like all basic truths it is a view which does not give the whole of the story.

For instance, it does not tell you how careful sponsors and others must be in the ultra-sensitive climate of today. A joke in one country gives mortal offence in another. Race relations, Women's Lib, animal rights, politics – these are all pitfalls for the sponsor.

The Benetton motor-racing supporters' club publishes a magazine called *Rabbit* which used to sport a leaping rabbit logo. There was a furore about testing perfumes on animals. Benetton's perfume, 'Colors', was accused of being tested on rabbits. A Benetton shop was fire-bombed in Italy. *Rabbit* dropped its logo!

Such problems apart, sports sponsors usually come under one of two categories: those who are seeking a good publicity and promotional outlet at the right price and are not much worried about which sport is involved; and those who have some enthusiasm for a particular sport and would like to help themselves by helping that particular sport.

For an Italian company such as Benetton, motor-racing was made to order. The Italians love motor-racing, have done so ever since it began, and when you are trying to sell exciting and colourful products what more glamorous sport could you find than motor-racing?

The Benetton story began in much more humble fashion in the 1960s when Luciano Benetton used a bicycle to deliver his sister's hand-knitted sweaters to customers in their homes in Northern Italy.

How that cottage industry grew into a multi-national business is one of the great commercial success stories of modern times. When one talks of franchise the American fast-food chains such as McDonald and Kentucky Fried Chicken come to mind. Benetton applied the franchise principle to its business and allowed individual store owners the right to sell the company's products. By the 1990s, Benetton was the world's leading knitwear producer and had expanded into other clothes markets, perfumes, banking and financial services. There were more than 4,000 Benetton outlets in 60 countries and an average of two franchises were opened every day.

Bright colours, vivid patterns and style-setting design are the Benetton hallmark and they were to influence the motor-racing operation. The familiar stitch logo became known world-wide as more than 40 million garments were sold each year. The retail outlets were all in the Benetton image, reflecting tasteful design standards – deliberately small, intimate shops, stacked neatly with vibrant colours.

An important plank in the marketing platform, it was felt, was to associate the company with the right images of life and style, bearing in mind that, in addition to Europe, products were exported in large quantities to the US, Japan and other countries.

Grand Prix racing with its colours, changes and glamour presented the perfect medium. In marketing terms alone, the Grands Prix present a unique opportunity – sixteen international events watched by over 1 billion people.

Benetton made their first entry into Grand Prix racing with Ken Tyrrell (seen here with his protégé, Jackie Stewart).

So – in 1983 – the die was cast. Benetton went into Grand Prix racing. It was a period of great change in the sport with teams gradually switching to turbo power and others clinging to the most successful engine in motor-racing history, the normally-aspirated Ford V8. Tyrrell was one of the latter teams and Benetton threw in their lot with Ken Tyrrell. According to reports, the basis of their agreement was a retainer, with performance-related bonuses.

The Tyrrell drivers were the Italian, Michele Alboreto, winner of the last 1982 Championship round at Las Vegas, and 33-year-old Kentuckian, Danny Sullivan, also a winner at Las Vegas but in the CANAM race which he won for the second year running. Sullivan, third in the CANAM Championship, had, rather surprisingly, taken up motor-sport twelve years previously – as a pupil at the Jim Russell Racing School at Snetterton in Norfolk.

At tests in Rio at the start of the season, Alboreto was fastest of the 'normal' cars and fifth fastest overall. Unfortunately, Alboreto was soon out of the Brazilian race after a collision with Mauro Baldi's Alfa Romeo but Sullivan drove steadily to finish eleventh.

Danny Sullivan who flitted briefly across the Benetton stage in the days when they were sponsoring the Tyrrell team returned to the States and greater glory, the highlight of his subsequent career being victory in the classic Indianapolis 500 Mile Race in 1985. The previous year he won the Cleveland, Pocono 500 and Sanair CART races; in 1985 he also won the Miami Indy Challenge; in 1986 he took the chequered flag at Meadowlands and Cleveland; in 1988 he won the CART/PPG Indy-car world series; and in 1989 he was first at Pocono again and Elkhart Lake. As the nineties dawned, the 40-year-old Kentuckian was still going strong.

When he quits racing, Sullivan may have another career beckoning – in films and TV. He has already appeared in the TV series 'Miami Vice' which stars Don Johnson and Philip Michael Thomas. Sullivan played a character called Danny Tepper – a race-driver, what else?

The Jim Russell Racing School which has trained so many good drivers sets up its recruiting 'stall' at Silverstone.

There was no joy for the team at Long Beach, a happy hunting ground for Tyrrell in the past, but hopes were still high as the teams moved back to Europe for the Race of Champions at Brands Hatch and the French Grand Prix on the Paul Ricard circuit. The latter was deemed a cert for the turbo cars owing to the nature of the circuit and so it proved but Sullivan was driving surely and of Alboreto's abilities there was no doubt.

Imola was another blank in so far as scoring Championship points was concerned, but a breakthrough came at Monaco when Sullivan, who had never driven the twisty street circuit before, brought his Benetton–Tyrrell into fifth place.

Testing at Spa saw Alboreto crash after one lap and the race itself did not provide much better fortune.

It was off to the US again and Ken Tyrrell expressed confidence – the Detroit circuit was ideal for the Ford engine, in his view, and Alboreto, who had won at Las Vegas the pre-vious year, just the man to win 'providing he keeps clear of the traffic jam on the first lap'.

That is just what he did. It was Alboreto's second Grand Prix win (and the motor-racing press said it endorsed the ability of Tyrrell, the man who put Jackie Stewart on the road to success, to pick driving talent); it was the third victory for a Ford engine in the 1983 season – all being on street circuits, Long Beach, Monaco and Detroit; it was the Ford engine's 155th win in Formula 1 World Championship races – and it would be six years before a Ford engine would win again.

Both the Benetton–Tyrrell cars finished in the top ten in Canada but this was a turbo bene-fit circuit again. The British, German and Aus-trian races told the same tale but at Zandvoort, Alboreto, driving a new car, the 012, did man-age to pick up a point in sixth place.

The Italian Grand Prix was another blank but the team went to Brands Hatch for the Grand Prix of Europe with some hope of gaining ad-vantage from the winding Kent circuit, a hope

Ken Tyrrell (far right) and his team after Jackie Stewart had been awarded the Segrave Trophy.

encouraged by the fact that earlier in the season, in the Race of Champions, Sullivan took a good second place on his first visit to the track. This time it was not to be. A broken oil line in Sullivan's No. 4 catching fire on lap 27 and the engine of Alboreto's No. 3 failing after 65 laps.

Thus the season finished in South Africa on something of a low note since this was Alboreto's last race before departing for the Ferrari team. He again had engine failure, this time on lap 60.

Sullivan, however, bowed out on a brighter note, finishing seventh and confirming yet again that he was far from a dud at this Grand Prix business.

For the Benetton family it could have been far worse. Alboreto had at least won in Detroit and that win was estimated to be worth $50 million in coast-to-coast US television exposure.

In summary, Benetton's first season of sponsorship had not been a bad one. Indeed some Formula 1 teams have less to show for umpteen seasons in World Championship racing.

Benetton-Tyrrell ended with one first, one fifth, one sixth, one seventh, three or four eighth places (depending upon how you do your counting – Alboreto and Sullivan tied for eighth in the Labatt Grand Prix of Canada), one ninth, one eleventh, two twelfth, one thirteenth and two fourteenth, a total of fifteen finishes and fifteen retirements. Unusually, six of the retirements were due to accidents, four of them involving Alboreto.

It could have been the beginning of a great partnership but it wasn't to be: entrants, sponsors and drivers all went their separate ways. Benetton decided to continue motor-racing sponsorship but for 1984 switched to an Italian team, the Alfa Romeo team run by Euroracing.

Alfa Romeo, after winning the first two World Drivers' Championships in 1950 and 1951, had withdrawn from Formula 1 racing until 1979 although they had supplied engines to March, McLaren and Brabham in the 1970s. Now, bearing the Benetton name, they had the Italian, Riccardo Patrese, and the American,

Eddie Cheever, as drivers. With a late start to the season (in March), Cheever took one of the cars into fourth position in the Brazilian Grand Prix behind Prost (McLaren), Rosberg (Williams) and De Angelis (Lotus). Patrese's gearbox went after 41 laps. The Alfas had blown no less than six engines in practice but Cheever drove a great race although only just beating Martin Brundle's Tyrrell, still Ford-powered.

It was Patrese's turn to finish fourth in South Africa, Cheever going out after 4 laps. Although both drivers had been worrying about fuel consumption, their engines blew up in the Belgian Grand Prix, Cheever's when the big American, again driving brilliantly, was in fifth place. Patrese suffered the same fate at Imola although Cheever did manage to get eighth place, running out of fuel when he was fifth.

Dijon and Monaco were blanks and in Canada poor old Cheever, once more lying fifth, ran out of fuel again and was classified twelfth. Detroit and Dallas went into the wastebin in so far as Benetton were concerned, Silverstone and Hockenheim followed. Patrese did manage to be classified in the Austrian race (tenth) although he wasn't running at the finish – out of fuel, as if you couldn't guess.

Engine trouble accounted for Patrese in the Netherlands, Cheever being classified fifteenth. Frantic work was going on behind the scenes and it was rewarded in the 'home' Italian Grand Prix with a third place for Patrese behind Lauda (McLaren) and Alboreto (Ferrari). Cheever was classified ninth having, surprise, surprise run out of fuel after 45 laps.

The European Grand Prix this year was held at the new Nürburgring. Patrese just squeezed into the sixth and last scoring spot, Cheever retiring with engine trouble after 37 laps. That was that, the season ending in Portugal with an eighth place for Patrese the best that the team could do.

Looking back at the season, Benetton must have reflected on what an extraordinary one it had been. This time they had been classified twelve times but on four of those occasions had actually run out of fuel before the finish. In two other races trouble with the fuel system and the metering unit had put the Alfas out. There were also five retirements due to accidents. Both Patrese and Cheever should remember the United States Grand Prix. The confines of JR's Dallas were too much for both men. Cheever swiped the wall on lap 8 and his Italian buddy followed suit 4 laps later.

Despite a third, a couple of fourth places and a sixth it had been far too uneven a season to hold out great hopes for the future – and so it proved. Alfas were on the downgrade, which happens to all race teams from time to time, and although Benetton did not sever their connections immediately they were still looking for the ideal mix. They turned to Toleman and for a while were associated with both teams. Around the Toleman tie-up they arranged a special promotion. 'United Colors of Benetton'.

The new partnership ran into difficulties right away, a dispute over securing a tyre contract delaying the launch of the Benetton-Toleman team until the fourth round of the championship at Monaco when Teo Fabi took part. The team was under the direction of Alex Hawkridge with Peter Collins as Team Manager and Rory Byrne as Designer. What happened to them in this somewhat ill-fated season has been described earlier but Benetton were not to be put off course. Midway through 1985 they took a step which they themselves described as stamping their character on a Grand Prix team of the future, combining the technical design talent of Rory Byrne; the perceptive managerial skills of Peter Collins; the energy of a closely-knit group of race staff; and the flair of talented, but young, Formula 1 drivers. The idea was to create a team with a completely fresh approach.

So, in 1986, a new company, Benetton Formula Limited, was established and the sponsors became owners and active participants, a rare step for sponsors to take. Toleman bowed out and Benetton took over the Witney establishment, the cars being built there and powered with BMW engines. They were driven by Gerhard Berger and Teo Fabi.

Berger won the 1986 Mexican Grand Prix, projecting the Benetton image around the world. Painted in strikingly different hues, the winning Benetton could hardly fail to attract attention. By 1988, Benetton had finished third in the World Championship behind McLaren and Ferrari. It easily defeated its non-turbo Formula 1 rivals and frequently beat its many more powerful turbocharged opponents.

McLaren–Honda won the 1988 World Championship with a turbocharged V6 engine but the Benetton Fords of Boutsen and Nannini

finished in the first three time and time again to make the team a clear third in the 1988 title race and first of the non-turbo teams.

In 1989 Nannini was retained for his second season with the team (owned by Luciano Benetton, together with his sister, Giulianna, and brothers Gilberto and Carlo). And, despite criticism of those who scoffed at taking on a young untried driver handicapped by injury, Luciano Benetton went along with the idea of Johnny Herbert occupying the driving seat of the second car. Confirming Herbert's appointment, Benetton described him as a 'driver that Peter Collins and Benetton have guided through the lower racing ranks and who is now poised for

Gancia sparkling wine, Riello industrial heating, Camel cigarettes and Mobil Oil are among the sponsors whose names adorn the Benetton cars. And the Fiesta is there as part of a promotion to encourage the young idea.

Racing enthusiasts are a ready market for all sorts of gear linked to their favourite teams. These postcards of the team drivers carry a facsimile signature on the reverse apart from the Benetton and Ford logos. And Mobil, Bulova, Cellnet, Camel, Riello, Nordica, Sanyo and Goodyear don't do so badly either.

Grand Prix stardom. Like Nannini, Herbert is a natural, a young driver hungry for success.'

Well, we all know what happened . . .

Benetton, nevertheless, have continued to put maximum effort into their motor-racing as into their products and outlets. In addition to the Benetton clothing division there are subsidiary companies for outdoor wear (Sisley), perfume (Colors de Benetton) and shoes (Divarese), all of them featured in racing activities. They are also featured in Benetton advertising on television and in newspapers and magazines. An ad boosting 'Colors: A New World For Men' aftershave and eau de toilette shows a clean fist and an oil-stained one meeting to hold a bottle of Colors and a offers a free scale model of the Benetton Formula 1 car with any two purchases.

Staff levels at the Witney factory are increasing and production space expanding. As a major technical partner, Ford continue to work with Benetton exclusively in Formula 1. Ford engines, built by Cosworth Engineering in England but with huge back-up support from Ford in both Europe and North America, make up a major commitment of time, technology and resources from the car-making giant.

As I write, Mobil continue to supply Benetton's fuel and oil, especially the Mobil 1 synthetic lubricant which has won three World

Championships. Goodyear, the most successful Formula 1 tyre-makers, supply Benetton with radials tailored to fit fast circuits and slow, wet and dry surfaces.

Indicating just what is entailed in putting a Grand Prix package together, other companies involved in the Benetton operation as the 1990s got under way included Motorola providing the team's radio communications set-up enabling conversation to take place against the roar of engines in the garage and for the pits to converse with drivers on the circuit.

Sanyo electronics, Camel cigarettes, 7-Up drinks, Gancia sparkling wine, Riello industrial central heating and Frizerga furnishings and design are others participating in a colourful (in every sense of the word) mixture appropriate to the most colourful cars in the Grand Prix circus.

An outstanding feature of Benetton since the day they first came into motor-racing has been an urgency to make progress, to look at every opportunity and to branch out, an attitude made very evident in September 1989, when Flavio Briatore confirmed a mid-season rumour, that John Barnard, rated by many the world's leading designer of Formula 1 cars, was leaving Ferrari to take up a new post as Technical Director of the Benetton Group of companies.

Barnard's brief was to establish a new high-technology research and development centre in the UK 'for the investigation, design and development of a wide ranging series of concepts for application in World Championship Formula 1 Grand Prix racing.' Put in plainer English, Barnard's team of engineers and scientists would be working on aerodynamcis, electronics, advanced materials, chassis and transmission design and suspension systems. They would be housed in a new centre, convenient to the Formula 1 team's headquarters at Witney, which would have its own wind tunnel, laboratories, test equipment and prototype production facilities.

Briatore said that Barnard would be given the opportunity of looking much further into the future than had previously been possible and

Brilliant British designer John Barnard whom Benetton recruited from Ferrari during 1989.

would be able to plan accordingly. His track record with McLaren and Ferrari placed him in a unique position. For 43-year-old Barnard it represented yet another challenge. At the same time he was probably relieved to be leaving Ferrari, a job which at one time, he freely admitted, threatened to destroy him.

After producing the all-conquering McLaren car, Barnard was, perhaps, on a hiding to nothing as they say in boxing. How do you go one better after designing the car which beat all-comers? There were obvious dangers about the Ferrari job. Italian temperament, internal politics, envy of a salary matching the top drivers — these were things expected to cause some problems.

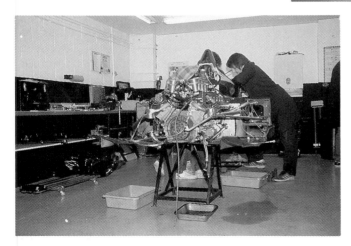

The Benetton factory at Witney which Benetton took over lock, stock and barrel from Toleman.

Others emerged . . .

Barnard's base remained in England which led to the Italian driver Michele Alboreto remarking that it was akin to a surgeon operating by telephone.

In 1989, Barnard introduced a semi-automatic seven-speed gearbox. Mansell won the opening race in Brazil but for the next five rounds neither car could finish and the critics had a field day. The cars were not only unreliable but unsafe, they chorused, pointing the finger at Berger's 'flamer' at Imola and Mansell's near-squeak in Monaco. Improvements to the gearbox and strengthening of the car itself had the desired effect. Mansell won in Hungary, Berger in Portugal and Barnard's reputation was vindicated.

Ferrari did make a bid to retain his services but Barnard opted for Benetton and a new challenge, a challenge which the security of a five-year contract guaranted him time enough to achieve something.

'I wouldn't be joining Benetton if I didn't think they could be up there with McLaren and Ferrari.'

CHAPTER 4

Nuts and Bolts

Michael Kranefuss is a German who lives in the United States with his wife, Imy, and two sons. He is often away from his home in Bloomfield Hills, Michigan, but wherever he goes he invariably takes a tennis racquet with him. When he is home he likes to sail and cycle.

So what? Well, unlikely as it may seem, the success or otherwise of the Anglo–Italian Benetton Ford racing team in the last decade of the twentieth century may well depend upon the decisions taken by this Americanized German. Truly, motor racing is an international sport . . .

The story really begins back in 1967, long before Benetton entered Grand Prix racing, and centres around a plain-speaking Englishman.

The 1961 to 1965 Grand Prix formula limited engines to a normally-aspirated 1.5-litre capacity and supercharging was not permitted. It was an era dominated by Jim Clark, the Scottish driver, and Lotus cars with the assistance of Coventry-Climax engines. BRM had at last achieved a degree of success and the availability of their engines plus those of Coventry-Climax kept the famed Coopers going and led to the formation of new teams like Brabham.

When the formula ended, the racing world was left in turmoil, at least in so far as engines were concerned. The new formula allowed for 3-litre engines, normally aspirated, or 1.5-litre supercharged. At this point, Coventry-Climax withdrew from racing and BRM announced that they were not in a position to supply engines in quantity.

The answers to the problem were many and manifold. That shrewd Australian, Jack Brabham, had seen what was coming and had made an agreement with Repco whose engine, although of limited power, was reliable and good enough to take the Brabham team to the World Championship. Ferrari, of course, had their own engines. The other teams were forced to use obsolete power units which conformed to the new regulations or develop new engines. A few 'bored out' 1.5-litre engines to their maximum capacity, about 2 litres, and made do with these. Oddly enough, these bored-out 2-litre engines did achieve some successes.

Only one man struck out bravely in a completely new direction. The Lotus boss, Colin Chapman, was determined to stay top of the Grand Prix tree, not only for his love of the sport but because his company was emerging as a manufacturer of high-speed quality cars – and motor-racing success was an influential factor in the sales graph.

He needed two things – the man to build a Grand Prix engine from scratch and the wherewithal to finance it. He knew the man already. His name was Keith Duckworth.

Duckworth was born in Blackburn, Lancashire, on 10 August 1933, son of a weaving shed owner, who died when the lad was twelve but not before he had passed on to his offspring some of his own practical engineering skills.

After boarding-school at Giggleswick, Yorkshire, young Duckworth did his National Service in the RAF, being discharged as the result of an injury – at rugby! He came to London and took an engineering course at the Imperial College, South Kensington, where he spent four years. The motor-racing bug bit in 1955 when he bought a Lotus in kit form, but his career as a racing driver was short-lived – three races in

The early sixties were dominated by Jim Clark and Lotus cars.

Although Jim Clark dominated the Grand Prix scene in the sixties he found time to rally with the Lotus Cortina, another link between competition motoring and production cars.

fact. He retired as an active driver after a race at Goodwood where 'I pushed the car through the chicane.' He realised he was not a natural race-driver and, sensibly, gave it up.

However, a connection, albeit tenuous, had been made with Lotus and during the college vacation he worked in the factory (then at Hornsey) alongside another young man named Graham Hill.

On leaving college, Duckworth applied to Lotus for a job as a development engineer and worked there for ten months, leaving (and this is interesting in the light of subsequent developments – no pun intended) after a policy disagreement. He had become friendly with another Lotus engineer, Mike Costin, and the

pair decided to set up their own company, Cosworth Engineering, christened from a combination of their own names.

The idea was that Duckworth would work full-time and Costin would put in as many hours as his duties at Lotus would allow. The company was formed in 1958 and almost simultaneously Colin Chapman appointed Mike Costin to the Lotus board and issued an edict that directors could not undertake outside work. So it was not until 1961 that 'Cos' joined up properly with 'worth'.

Costin developed the Lotus Formula Junior car while Duckworth used the popular Ford 105E engine as a basis upon which to build a Formula Junior engine. Team Lotus bought all

Keith Duckworth, designer of the Ford DFV Formula 1 engine, at his drawing-board.

Duckworth with the engine itself.

its Formula Junior engines from Duckworth and it proved a considerable success, naturally attracting the attention of the Ford Motor Company. Ford then gave some help to Duckworth in developing a highly successful Formula 2 engine.

And that was the situation when Chapman came to his Rubicon. Colin was an adventurous man (he must have been – he once sounded out the present writer about taking over his press and PR department), too adventurous, perhaps, in view of the events which clouded the latter part of his life. Now he went after every likely bod in search of the necessary finance to enable Duckworth to create a world-beating Grand Prix engine. The Government, no less. But the dead hand of Whitehall did not even quiver. Just the thumb moved downwards. The Society of Motor Manufacturers and Traders, the David Brown Organization, British Sound Recording and others were more enthusiastic but for various reasons no deal took place.

One night, Chapman invited Walter Hayes, Ford's dynamic PR man, to dinner. Hayes put Chapman's finance proposals to Ford's engineering chief, an American named Harley Copp, he put it to the boss man, another American

named Stanley Gillen – and Chapman had his finance.

Ironically, the decision which was to have the most far-reaching effects in motor-racing history was taken at a board meeting under the heading, 'Any Other Business'. It has to be one of the best decisions that even a giant corporation like Ford has ever taken and it was certainly one of the most painless – no arguments, just a few words and the deed was done.

In the new engine's first season, 1967, Jim Clark's Lotus won the Dutch, British, US and Mexican Grands Prix. By the following season, McLaren and Matra had joined Lotus in using the engine and between them the three marques won eleven Grand Prix races. Brabham and March followed and then Tyrrell. Later on, the short-lived Wolf team would also be Ford-Cosworth powered as well as the French team of Guy Ligier.

It was to Wolf that the honour of scoring the engine's 100th victory would fall. On 22 May 1977, the South African, Jody Scheckter, drove his Wolf-Ford across the finishing line to win the Monaco Grand Prix after leading all the way. It had been ten years since the engine was conceived and just seven units built to power one marque, the Lotus.

The Ford DFR Formula 1 engine.

The Ford 3.5 litre V8 Formula 1 engine.

The South African, Jody Scheckter chalked up the Ford Formula 1 engine's 100th victory when he won the 1977 Monaco Grand Prix in a Wolf-Ford.

On 15 August 1982, another landmark was reached. Elio de Angelis (Lotus-Ford) won the Austrian Grand Prix by a few feet from Keke Rosberg (Williams-Ford). It was the driver's first Grand Prix win, the first win for Lotus in four years and the 150th World Championship victory for the Ford DFV engine.

The following year saw Benetton come on the scene, sponsoring the Tyrrell team, a team with a fine record in Formula 1. Benetton-Tyrrell won the US Grand Prix in 1983 but that was to be the last Ford victory for six years because the turbos were taking over and normally-aspirated power units were outclassed.

It probably did not worry Benetton too much. They had switched attention to Alfa Romeo in 1984 and when, eventually, they took over the Toleman team at Witney it was to use BMW engines with which they won their second Grand Prix, the Mexican, in 1986.

Which is where the German connection came in . . .

Ford and Benetton as companies are not the sort to rest on their laurels. Keith Duckworth as an individual constantly seeks perfection. And Michael Kranefuss is of the same mould. A native of Munster, Westphalia, he used to hitch-hike from his home to the Nürburgring in the 1950s to watch the top racers. Then he began to compete, often driving Ford Escorts.

Elio de Angelis's first Grand Prix win – for Lotus-Ford in the 1982 Austrian Grand Prix – was the 150th World Championship victory for Ford engines.

In addition to Ford, he also drove Fiat Abarth, Alfa Romeo and BMW and, in all, drove professionally for six years in international events.

In 1966 Michael became manager of the planned Sauerland Ring racing circuit project in the eastern part of North Rhine-Westphalia. In 1968 he joined Ford of Germany's newly-formed Competitions Department and, in 1972, was appointed Motor Sport Manager. That was the year Ford scored a major success with first three places in the 24-hour Race at Spa. From 1971 through 1976 Ford Capris won the German Production Car Championship for six straight years and the European Touring Car Championship three times.

Michael was appointed Ford of Europe's Motor Sport Director in 1976, a position he held until he moved to the US in September 1980, to become the company's Director of

Michael Kranefuss, the American-based German who heads Ford's Special Vehicle Operations including the Grand Prix activities.

69

Special Vehicle Operations. During this time he was responsible for the highly successful Ford of Britain Escort rally team under the management of Peter Ashcroft which, in 1979, won the World Rally Championship.

In his new job Kranefuss was responsible for the liaison between Benetton and Ford and so Benetton ran in 1987 with Ford V6 turbos. The team was fairly consistently amongst the leaders, scoring Championship points in ten of the sixteen rounds including third places in Austria and Australia and being placed fifth in the Constructors' Championship.

(The Data General Tyrrell team, equipped with the normally-aspirated Ford-Cosworth DFZ 3.5-litre engine, won the Colin Chapman Trophy for cars in this category.)

With the turbo era coming to an end, Ford, Cosworth and Benetton put their heads to-

Peter Ashcroft, manager of the Ford Rally Team which won the 1979 World Championship.

gether. They decided to race in 1988 using a normally-aspirated engine, the 3.5-litre DFR; this prior to the completely new engine, being developed by Cosworth, being available for 1989.

As with the DFZ, the DFR was developed from the original 3-litre DFV but was designed to accept a number of additional features as the season wore on. These included: different valve arrangements; the five-valves per cylinder head which was developed by Yamaha for the 3-litre DFV racing in Formula 3000 in Japan; a new crankcase design which reduced the overall height of the engine; a number of different electronic systems and a new generation of Ford engine management systems which would be used in the 1989 engines and also in future Ford production engines.

In fact, most of the amendments were intended to be tested for possible use in the 1989 engine. For the first 1988 race, along with the new crankcase an experimental four-valve per cylinder arrangement was used, together with a new fuel system designed by Cosworth. Further valve arrangements, including the five-valve-head and alternative engine components would be tested on a race-to-race basis. The bottom line was that at mid-season a final decision would be made as to the configuration of the 1989 engine.

At the time Kranefuss said:

'We're entering 1988 with two engines and three programmes: the DFZ Ford-Cosworth, the four- and five-valve DFR and initial layouts for an all-new 3.5-litre engine for 1989–90. As everybody knows, our principal contribution to Grands Prix since we entered this arena in 1967 has been in the provision of power to competing teams. We remain committed to this in the long term and continue to see it as our duty to provide the means with which other people can go racing.'

The experiments in 1988 could not have gone too badly since drivers Nannini and Boutsen logged sixteen Championship scoring places between them.

Despite the usual teething troubles the 1989 engine eventually saw the light of day. What a contrast everything was from the old days of Grand Prix racing when often the difference between winning and losing was the ability or lack of it of an oil-stained mechanic with a spanner. With this engine, Ford Scientific Research groups in both Europe and North America had assisted in developing special materials for the construction and the Ford Electrical and Electronics Operations designed and developed the engine's electronic management and fuel systems. Transatlantic computer links would be used to enable data to be analysed and evaluated at any time of day and night.

All very different from the old days of one mechanic yelling to another, 'Ave yer got any of those new spark plugs, Nobby?'

Great attention had been paid to keeping the engine compact. It was just 20.5in (52.1cm) high, 23.3in (59.1cm) wide and 23.4in (59.5cm) long, which, of course, is helpful to the car designer. (Of which more later.)

The 1988 engine weighed 308lb (140kg) and Cosworth set out to achieve weight savings on this. Special aluminium alloys were used in the construction of cylinder heads, cylinder block and sump; magnesium alloy for the cam box covers and carbon-fibre for the fuel injection system's air intakes. Components within the engine were manufactured from steel, titanium and a number of advanced specification alloys.

Operating at a compression ratio of 12:1 the engine had two inlet and two exhaust valves per cylinder operated by twin overhead camshafts on each bank of cylinders. At the 1989 stage of development, the power output was over 600hp.

The engine management system, primarily developed for use on production cars, could handle more than 1 million commands per second and was claimed to be totally responsible for the engine's operating strategy, tailoring engine performance to the particular needs of circuits, weather and track conditions.

Win that World Championship soon, Nigel, you're not going to be needed much longer.

Commenting on Ford's more-than-thirty-years relationship with Cosworth, Michael Kranefuss emphasized that the partnership had been responsible for a continuing flow of thoroughbred road engines, apart from the Grand Prix and rally engines. He said:

'Formula 1 continues to command world-wide attention and be the most demanding and competitive of all racing formulae and it helps us to promote Ford and its products internationally. But it also enables us to research and develop an increasing range of electronics, materials and power train components for production vehicles.'

The disappearance of the turbo in 1989 meant that thirteen of the Grand Prix teams were Ford-powered but only Benetton, in the latter half of the season, had the new engine. The other twelve – Arrows, Rial, AGS, Tyrrell, Minardi, BMS Dallara, Eurobrun, Ligier, Osella, Coloni, Onyx and FIRST – had to make do with the 1988 version.

Subsequently it was announced that Benetton would have the exclusive use of the new engine through 1990 and 1991 with an option for 1992, a disappointment to some teams who had hoped to be allowed 'off the shelf' engines while Benetton continued to have exclusive use of the latest development engines. For Benetton it enhanced the potential of the next few years.

Engines are not much use without a chassis to put them in and the man who has played the biggest part in the design of Benetton cars up to 1990 is a remarkable fellow who has been three times a World Champion himself – at hand-launch gliding. Rory Byrne is of Irish stock (with a name like that, what else?) but was born and brought up in in Pretoria, South Africa.

He won the gliding championship in 1961, 1962 and 1964 but gradually racing cars took more of his time and in 1973 he arrived in England to help a friend race in Formula Ford.

Rory Byrne, South African-born glider champion, who turned out to be a bright racing car design talent with Benetton.

Modifications made by Rory to the Royale RP16 were so successful that Royale offered him the post of Chief Designer which he accepted, thus beginning a very good four-year association, both for the small British company and for its Chief Designer. Along the way Byrne worked on Rad Dougall's championship-winning Formula Ford 2000 car and so, when Dougall and his backers, the Toleman Group, wanted to run a March-BMW in Formula 2, Rory was the obvious choice.

Totally absorbed in car design, Rory speedily learned about this competitive international formula and so he was well prepared when Toleman decided to build their own cars for the 1980 season. Brian Henton, driving Rory Byrne's Toleman-Hart, duly won the European Championship that year.

Formula 1 was the logical step for the team from Witney and Rory was cast into the deep end with the Toleman-Hart TG181, one of the first turbocharged cars in Grand Prix racing.

What happened then has already been told but the years after Benetton succeeded Toleman were days and weeks and months of furious activity, the unavoidable changing of engines calling for a re-design of the cars and the exercising of Byrne's skills. He had hardly finished the B188, his fourth new car in as many years, than he was hard at work on the B189.

The B188 just *had* to be a completely new car since not only did it involve the switch from a turbo to a normally-aspirated engine but there had been a regulation change which required the driver's feet to be placed behind the front-centre axle line of the car.

Benetton backroom boy, Dave Wass, is one of the most experienced designers in the business. He was one of the original members of Arrows, mainly ex-employees of Shadow and had previously been with BRM.

The first Arrows was built in sixty days but Don Nichol, boss of Shadow, in a successful court action, claimed it was built from designs of Wass and Tony Southgate when they were employed by him.

Many people do not know how the name Arrows originated and are confused by the 's' on the end. The team was named after its founders: Franco and Christine **A**mbrosie, Alan **R**ees, Jackie **O**liver, Dave **W**ass and Tony **S**outhgate.

Rory and his henchmen, Dave Wass (one time Chief Designer for Arrows) and Paul Crooks, set to work. As Rory says:

'It meant a fundamentally different car. The mounting of the engine was similar to the turbo and the rear suspension arrangement was much the same as before but there were substantial revisions to the weight distribution.

'Instead of suspending the gearbox at the very back of the car, it was positioned between the engine and the rear axle line. That change, plus the fact that the gears themselves could be smaller because of the reduction in torque, meant designing and developing a completely new transmission system.

'At the front we also had to make a major revision. We had to meet the regulation changes but also I wanted to retain our distinctive needle nose so the spring/damper units were situated under the driver's heels and the springs and dampers operated by a bell crank activated by pull rods. We thought it beneficial in terms of overall layout.

'We also looked closely at everything which might improve the aerodynamic efficiency of the entire car.'

The total length of the car was 182in (462.2cm), height 38in (96.5cm) and width 55in (140cm).

Hardly had the design team mopped the sweat from their brows and sharpened their pencils than it was on with the next car, the B189 which had to be designed so as to accommodate the new 75-degree Ford V8 which, at least, was lighter and more compact than the Ford DFR engine it was to replace.

This car was very much a result of close co-operation between the car and engine designers. Rory explains:

'A lot of thought was put into it at the design/concept stage, and we were able to do a great deal of research into the engine-chassis relationship rather than spending our time as so often is the case in working out how to adapt an existing engine design. As a result we were able to produce a neater, lighter package right on the weight limit.

'We were able to take advantage of the fact that both the engine and the car were totally new. With the B188 the design parameters were largely dictated by the change to the regulations and a switch to the existing engine. With the B189 we were able to develop the fundamentally sound principles from the B188 and yet introduce a lot of new ideas at the same time. It was a pleasure to be able to work that way for a change.'

Extensive wind tunnel work led to improvements in aerodynamic efficiency and although the transmission layout remained as before, modifications produced a reduction in mechanical losses through the drive train. The steering rack was located ahead of the front axle line and the seating position lowered – only possible in the absence of a big driver. And a Ford electronic system meant that every aspect of the car's performance could be monitored continuously throughout every race, qualifying and test session.

What next? Why the B190 of course, powered by the 1990 derivative of the Ford engine. Both were track testing by September, 1989, looking to the season ahead.

Deep in contemplation: Benetton Team Manager Gordon Message even forgets to light his cigarette.

Yet all this technology has not made the backroom boys of motor sport – the team managers, technicians and mechanics – redundant. Benetton Ford, like all Grand Prix teams, still have to rely upon the Peter Collins and Gordon Messages of this world, Rory Byrne, John Gentry (one-time Shadow designer), Dave Wass, Nigel Stepney, Paul Crooks, Pat Symonds (a survivor of the Toleman days), Pat Fry and the rest of the gang. These are the boys who still work long unsociable hours, fly and drive many thousands of miles during the season and still manage to keep smiling. Well, at least some of the time.

With Fords back in the winning lane, perhaps some thoughts on design and life would not come amiss from the man who, in effect, began the Ford engine success story, Keith Duckworth:

'Development is only necessary due to the ignorance of designers.'

'First ideas usually turn out to be complicated: a lot more design thought is required to get the same result simply.'

'Computers cannot think, therefore they cannot design.' (Or presumably, drive. Nigel, Sandro and Nelson should be pleased about that.)

'Thought should be encouraged rather than systems made to avoid it – otherwise all progress will cease.'

'I don't agree with free expression. I believe that man is inherently idle. He must be prompted now and again. There has to be discipline. People need to jump.' As someone else commented, racing cars need to 'jump' too. No one has prompted them to jump more than Keith Duckworth.

His achievement in winning 100 Grand Prix races was marked by the Royal Automobile Club (RAC) with its premier award, the Diamond Jubilee Trophy. In receiving it, Keith said, 'My approach to design is very fundamental – faced with a problem I attempt to analyse the requirement.' In the case of the Grand Prix engine, Duckworth got it right first time.

The new regulations for Grand Prix engines which came into force in 1989 were expected to remain fundamentally unchanged until the year 2000 although no one with any knowledge of motor racing would care to bet on it.

A maximum limit of twelve cylinders was imposed and engines had to be 3½-litre normally-aspirated four-strokes, with a stipulation that cylinders must be circular in cross-section. By ruling out oval pistons the authorities had ensured that the number of cylinders chosen for an engine would be more critical than usual in determining size and weight.

The regulations left Formula 1 engine designers with three alternatives, none with clear-cut advantages. On the contrary, each had both advantages and disadvantages when compared with the other two. The choices were:

1. V8 cylinder layout to give maximum compactness.
2. V12 to give maximum revs and power.
3. V10, a compromise between the two.

A think tank of Keith Duckworth, Dick Scammell, Martin Walters and Chief Designer Geoffrey Goddard were left to make the decision. It was not an easy one and discussions went on for several months, aided by Goddard's proposals for possible layouts for each choice. In April 1988, the decision was finally taken to make the new engine another V8.

A number of factors prompted this decision.

Compactness, of course, was a main one. It was of even more importance now that the regulations demanded that the driver's feet should not extend beyond the centre line of the front wheels. This meant, in effect, that the cockpit had to be located further back within the wheelbase.

Complementary to the compactness of a V8 engine was a saving in weight which gave some help to the car's designers in effecting the best weight distribution, always a difficult task when the heaviest components of a modern race car are all located behind the driver.

Despite its compact nature, the V8 cylinder block is long enough to accommodate externally the various pumps, drives and so on, with a minimum interference to airflow whilst still having the advantage over the V10 or V12 that its shorter length allows more space for the fuel tank or gives more flexibility to the length of the wheelbase.

Funnily enough, not all of the work on the turbo was wasted. Believe it or not, the new V8 had more in common with the 1½-litre turbo than it did with the 3½-litre DFR, particularly as regards internal construction. It was because much of the design and development work which went into the turbo engine could also be applied to the new one that the V8 was designed and built in far shorter time than would normally have been the case.

Mark you, it was still not produced without exceptional effort by a lot of people. Geoff Goddard and his staff produced more than 500 working drawings, the Cosworth foundries, forge and machine shops and the prototype-build department all worked round the clock — and outside contractors such as the pattern makers were so carried away by everyone's enthusiasm that they increased their normal working hours by as much as 75 per cent. Which belies the impression often given in newspapers and on television that the British working man no longer exists or, at least if he does, he no longer wants to work.

The first of the new engines went on dynamometer test the week before Christmas 1988, in effect the fourth new Formula 1 engine to be introduced in as many years and a remarkable achievement by all concerned. With more than a touch of pride in his voice, Dick Scammell gave his opinion that no other organization in the world could have coped with such a schedule so successfully. It would be a brave or foolish man who denies him. And as Benetton-Ford aim for Grand Prix glory in the final decade of the twentieth century that organization is still there working to make the team a highly successful one.

Although Keith Duckworth has retired as Chairman of the company his services are still available as a consultant. His original partner, Mike Costin, the 'Cos' of Cosworth, is now Chairman of the board but not greatly involved in the racing side. He is concerned primarily with passenger car operations such as the Sierra RS Cosworth engine.

Both 'Cos' and 'Worth' like flying but whereas Mike Costin loves gliding, his old pal prefers helicopters. If urgent business demands it, Mike will pilot himself in the company's Cessna 172.

The Formula 1 activities are now the responsibility of Dick Scammell, Director of Racing, and it would be hard to find a more experienced man. His involvement in racing goes back more than three decades since he joined Team Lotus as a mechanic in 1960. Two years later he became personal mechanic to the late great Jim Clark and in 1965 was promoted to Chief Mechanic of Lotus. In 1968 he was made Lotus Racing Manager.

He left the Chapman organization in 1971 to organize the restoration of 40 racing cars which were to form the nucleus of Tom Wheatcroft's museum and to supervise the rehabilitation of the Donington circuit which by then Tom owned. Dick joined Cosworth the following year as Development Department Manager but stayed only two years, the challenge of setting up the Vels Parnelli Jones team, a new Formula 1 name, being too much for him. But, in 1976, he returned to Cosworth – and stayed there. He has been closely involved in both Formula 1 and Indianapolis engine development ever since and became Director of Racing in 1986.

Off-duty – which isn't very often – Dick Scammell's idea of a rest from work is . . . restoring two historic sports cars which he owns. But he isn't averse to a spot of sailing.

> The first Cosworth USAC engine was used by Al Unser in the final race of the 1975 American season. In 1977, Unser, Rutherford, Sneva, Ongais and Andretti all drove Cosworth-powered cars and between them, in fourteen races, had eight wins, seven seconds and five thirds, the start of an American success story which was to rival Cosworth's achievements in Grand Prix racing.

Geoff Goddard, as Chief Designer, is Keith Duckworth's true descendant in racing engine terms and the new engine is his baby just as much as the original engine and its variations was Keith's. Geoff literally knocked on the Cosworth door and asked for a job back in 1971. Rolls-Royce aero engines, where he worked as an apprentice, had collapsed, leaving Geoff and many others redundant. Duckworth himself took him on and eventually Geoff worked closely with 'the master', By the time Ford returned to Formula 1 with the 1½-litre turbo, Geoff was in charge of engine design.

Completing the powerful Cosworth team is Martin Walters, the Chief Development Engineer who, like Scammell, has had two spells with Cosworth, the first commencing in 1967. Then, after six years with March, he returned in 1978 to take up his present post.

A deciding factor in many a Grand Prix has been tyres. Burst tyres, worn tyres, wrong decisions re-using wet or dry tyres, slow or fast tyre changes by the pit crews . . . all of these can influence the final result.

Benetton, as with a dozen other Grand Prix teams, have been running on Goodyear these several seasons and Goodyear proudly proclaimed at the end of 1989 that every World Championship Formula 1 Grand Prix had been won on their tyres.

In the old days, it used to be said that the main purpose of motor-racing was 'improving the breed', testing new developments which ultimately would go into the ordinary motor car. With the massive commercialization of today's motor-sport, cynics tend to deride this theory but it is still a fact that improvements in racing often lead to benefits in production cars.

This is especially true when it comes to tyres. Although when one looks at the strange objects worn by Grand Prix cars today it is difficult to see any resemblance to the tyres on the family saloon, nevertheless, the experimental work which has gone into materials and design for racing bring great benefit for ordinary tyre production. A tyre which can withstand all the forces and stresses of Grand Prix racing should certainly be able to withstand the perils of the school and shopping run and annual jaunt to France.

Most of the great names in tyre manufacture are, or have been, associated with racing at one time or another – Michelin, Dunlop, Firestone, Pirelli and so on.

Goodyear – named after the man who evolved 'vulcanization' by mixing rubber and sulphur to make rubber a thoroughly adaptable and consistent product – was not founded as a company until 1898. This being nearly forty

Tyres and wheels stockpiled at the back of the pits.

Michelin crew hard at work during a test day at Brands Hatch.

years after Goodyear, the inventor, had died in a New York hotel room, broken-hearted by the death of his daughter and $200,000 in debt. Naming the company after him was a belated recognition of the contribution he had made to mankind's health, comfort and efficiency.

(Why 'vulcanization'? After Vulcan, the Roman god of fire. Goodyear discovered his process when he dropped a piece of rubber, mixed with sulphur, on the stove at his home and it charred just like leather.)

The Goodyear company's involvement with the Grand Prix scene goes back more than 25 years; in 1965 Richie Ginther scored Goodyear's first victory, winning the Mexican Grand Prix at the wheel of a 'works' Honda. Yet the basic theory on which the Goodyear racing tyre design is based, now known as Neutral Contour Technology, was originally developed more than 60 years ago by one of their engineers, John Purdy. The theory is that if the internal stresses within a tyre can be equalized, then an optimum balance in ride and handling can be achieved, which, in plain, simple English,

A bystander scratches his head as race tyres go by apparently under their own steam.

means that a car's performance can be significantly improved if more of its tyre tread can be placed firmly on the road.

Modern computer technology has enabled Purdy's theory to be developed to the optimum. In the field of racing tyres it led to the very successful low-profile Formula 1 tyre, the Eagle F1, which has a directional tread so designed as to get rid of the maximum amount of water when racing on a thoroughly wet circuit. This directional tread was then adapted so as to provide good wet-weather tyres for fast production cars.

In addition to supplying Honda, Goodyear also provided tyres for Brabham in 1965. Through this association with the Australian and his team, they won their first World Championship the following year.

Another title followed in 1967, again with Brabham. Then, with a number of rival tyre manufacturers active in the sport, a full-scale 'war' developed, one of the consequences being the ever-increasing width of the tyres, as any 'before and after' photographs will show. In 1965 Goodyear tyres had a tread-width of 5in. By the end of the season they were 6in and, in 1966, 7½in. At the beginning of 1968 the new Goodyear tyres were 11½in and, by the middle of the season, Dan Gurney's Eagles were running on rear tyres with a tread 13½in wide.

When Tyrrell joined the Goodyear camp in 1971, the tyre company found a great tyre test-driver in Jackie Stewart and so began an association which was to last long after the 'wee man' had retired as an active driver.

The other significant happening that season was the appearance of 'slick' tyres, tyres with no real tread pattern, an idea derived from

American drag racing and made possible by the advances in tread compounds and internal construction. These tyres, of course, were a great help on dry circuits although sudden downpours of rain could catch cars out, resulting in sliding all over the road. Many a gamble was taken on whether or not to start a race on dry or wet weather tyres.

World Championships continued to be associated with Goodyear. Stewart produced a couple for them and so did Emerson Fittipaldi with McLaren. Then for a while Goodyear found itself the only tyre company directly involved in Grand Prix racing but continued to support the sport and carry out a full development programme. The monopoly did not last long but, despite competition, Goodyear-shod teams won the Championship in 1978, 1980, 1981, 1982, 1983, 1985, 1986, 1987, 1988 and 1989.

Today, with thirteen teams to service, the task of transporting Goodyear tyres to sixteen races all over the world is a mammoth one. Six articulated transporters are used and some 2,300 Eagle F1 radial racing tyres are taken to each World Championship event, accompanied by twenty-two Goodyear Racing Division personnel including management, public relations staff, engineers and tyre-fitters.

The actual tyres taken will depend upon a number of factors. There is a whole range of compounds, but normally only two compounds

Goodyear and other tyre manufacturers devote a lot of research into getting rid of water, but sometimes a wet track can provide an artistic scene as in this shot of Stefan Belloff.

will be taken. Which two will depend upon the track surface and length, the anticipated weather conditions and so on. Circuits fall roughly into one of three categories: low-grip street circuits such as Monaco and Phoenix; medium-speed tracks such as Estoril; and high-speed tracks like Silverstone – and not too many others.

In addition to the two compounds chosen, ultra-soft tyres will also be taken. These will usually last for only one to three laps but are used in qualifying to get maximum results.

Temperature factors may affect the choice of compound. So may driver preference. There is no automatic reason why harder compound cannot be used on one side of the car, softer on the other. But the tyre engineers are always on hand to make sure that whatever the tyre choice and set-up it makes sense and will not leave the team or the tyre manufacturer looking stupid.

All the data from each Grand Prix is fed into the ubiquitous computers and stored in memory banks and, in addition to the racing itself, Goodyear run regular test days throughout the year, irrespective of season. Nevertheless, the Grand Prix remains the most important cog in the machine, its value as a testing ground being that it pushes the construction of tyres and their materials to the outer limit of performance. If a tyre is satisfactory under racing conditions, it will work under normal circumstances with a considerable safety margin in hand. So the Formula 1 tyre on the Benetton today may be the forebear of the one on a Ford Fiesta tomorrow.

Goodyear's Director of International Racing, Leo Mehl, sums it all up thus:

'There is no question in my mind we are the Number 1 tyre company in Grand Prix racing and we intend to stay that way. However, we welcome competition from other tyre companies in Formula 1 because the benefits which accrue from this business are split pretty well 50–50 between the technical feedback and the advertising benefit. But you run the danger of losing both if you don't have the stimulus of competition. Goodyear has a long-term commitment to this business.'

It certainly is a bigger commitment than when Goodyear began its racing programme at Wolverhampton, England, in 1964. Although FISA lays down restrictions on tyre sizes, those sizes are still way above those of a quarter-century ago. The overall width when fitted and inflated is now up to 18in. The rear tyres are usually made to the maximum, the fronts slightly smaller. There is a restriction of 26in on the overall diameter.

And, if you wonder how the tyre pressures compare with your own runabout, the answer is 18–20psi at the front, 16–18psi at the rear.

The impression should not be left that all tyre testing takes place in the lab or during actual races. Earlier it was mentioned that Jackie Stewart was a great tyre test-driver and, in modern racing too, most drivers take part at some time or another in the test sessions which are held at all the major tracks so as to develop tyres which will exactly suit the characteristics of that particular circuit. Such sessions are known as 'seat of the pants testing', the testing that no machine can ever take over – no computer can replace that vital connection between the seat of the pants and the human brain.

When it comes to the crucial question of the 'feel' of a tyre, whether it is a road tyre that is never going over 70mph or 80mph or a racing tyre designed to run at three times the speed, Goodyear say that no instruments can give you information that you can glean from a skilled test driver.

It does not necessarily follow that a good Grand Prix driver is a very good test-driver. A lot are – Stewart was a fine example – and when Benetton signed Nelson Piquet they did have in mind that the Brazilian would be a great help in testing apart from his deeds in competition proper. Some drivers, however, lack the ability to dissect a car's performance whether it be

Tyre companies valued the knowledge of Niki Lauda – here with his Goodyear-shod McLaren (above) *and winning the British GP running on Michelin* (below).

chassis, engine or tyres and convey worthwhile information to the mechanics and backroom boys. Some make no bones about it – the Swiss driver Gregor Foitek, for instance. 'It is difficult for me to explain to the engineers what the car is doing exactly, and how to change it.' Other drivers, not good enough to hold down a regular Grand Prix drive, are still first-class on the testing side. Emanuele Pirro, for example, who had a half-season with Benetton and did not pull up any trees, is yet highly regarded by Honda as a test driver.

Goodyear's Racing Division today regard testing as a more important part of their work than ever before. The dependence on feedback from the driver is just one similarity between the testing techniques used on the race circuit and those used on Goodyear's testing grounds, like the one at the massive Test Centre at Colmar-Berg in Luxemburg.

The top racing drivers – and where Good-

Mario Andretti, one of the stars who is regarded by the technicians as a fine test driver.

Goodyear tyre technicians at work in the Benetton pits.

Ford's Flat-Trac tyre test equipment in use at the Dunton research establishment. This company was first in Europe to use this equipment (in 1984), ahead even of European tyre manufacturers.

year is concerned these have included Niki Lauda and Mario Andretti in addition to Stewart – have the same approach to their job as the drivers on the company's tyre test-fleet. They must take the tyre to the limits of its capability while at the same time assessing its characteristics and judging the effect on the car's handling. They must be able to make this assessment whilst driving at top speed and not wait for the bang to deduce that something is wrong! And then, which is where some drivers have difficulty, they must be able to report their findings clearly to the engineers when they come back into the pits.

The stop-watch is the other important factor

in race tyre testing. Lap times are measured in hundredths of a second and a tyre which will make a car go a couple of tenths of a second faster per lap is a real achievement. So at race tyre test-sessions timings are to a tenth of a second.

Machines and recording devices do, of course, play their part in tyre testing and in this area the racers have learned from the road testers. The trend towards miniaturization which is so much a part of modern technology has made it possible to make measuring devices much more compact – for example, recorders which would previously only fit into the boot of a passenger car are now small enough to be carried on a Formula 1 car. Goodyear has gained a great deal of knowledge about vehicle behaviour from its experiments with fully instrumented racing cars. A side product is that the strain placed upon measuring devices being operated at racing speeds has brought about changes in the instruments themselves which in turn have improved their dependability for normal testing.

There is one area, however, where both road and racing tyres have to leave the test-tracks behind and come inside. That is destruction testing where a tyre is deliberately taken to and beyond its limits of performance. The wheel fitted with the test-tyre is set against a dynamometer, a large rotating wheel, and the speed of this large wheel is increased until the tyre is turning at such a speed that its construction can

no longer hold up and it fails. That failure speed is always well above the designated safe speed of both road and racing tyres but the information gained is invaluable in 'improving the breed'.

Yet, with all the machines and stop-watches, in the final analysis the machine can only tell you so much and there is still a requirement for that vital connection between the seat of the pants and the brain.

Benetton now have the engine, the chassis, the tyres. What else is required? Lubricant, of course. And the current Benetton Ford power plants, turning out more than 625bhp at 11,000-plus rpm, are totally lubricated by Mobil 1. That includes Mobil 1 Formula 15W–50 in the engine.

What is amazing is that these man-made oils out-perform the best that nature can produce. A

The tyre companies get return on their Grand Prix investment in research, sales and – as seen here – publicity.

conventional lubricant starts with crude oil. A series of refinery processes leaves several thousand kinds of hydrocarbons that work together . . . more or less. But they also include some ingredients not ideal for lubrication or which create a problem at extreme temperatures, wax for example. In contrast, Mobil 1 is put together from a few pure chemical 'building blocks' chosen for their special lubricating ability and minus any wax. Thus at one extreme, $-37.2°C$ ($-35°F$)/$300°C$ ($570°F$), when most conventional oils are virtually solid, the man-made synthetic oil will flow easily, retaining its lubricating ability and pumping quickly to where it's needed. Since even Bernie Ecclestone has not yet thought of running an Antarctic Grand Prix, sponsored by Glacier Mints, Benetton are not too greatly concerned about what happens at freezing point and below but Mobil 1 continues to flow easily, retaining heat and lubricating ability up through $300°C$ ($570°F$), at which point many conventional oils have started to break down.

The synthetic oil's superior stability over a wider temperature range takes on crucial significance as designers increasingly get more power out of smaller engines working faster – and hotter.

These Mobil synthetic lubricants have already more than proved their worth in motor-racing. In the Grand Prix World Championship they had, by 1989, contributed to seven Drivers' and Constructors' titles. In the US, in 1988 alone, they contributed to five US driver championships and 67 races in events ranging from stock production cars to 725bhp, 230mph, Indianapolis 500 cars.

As with tyre research and development, synthetic lubricants are using motor-racing to help in other fields. This modern technology now meets the demands of space craft, nuclear submarines, commercial jet airliners, military aircraft, commercial transport – all concerns seeking economy of operation and industrial equipment which require high-speed, high-temperature operation in order to produce at top efficiency.

The bottom line, of course, is that you don't just have to watch the pit crew putting Mobil 1 into Nannini's car or Piquet's, you can buy it for your own car on your local garage forecourt.

'Man-made oil beats nature's best' is a slogan which would have had them muttering 'Must be mad' in the Paddock at Brooklands in the salad days of British motor-racing. In those days and for a long time to come, there was always a pungent smell around a racetrack, the smell emanating from car exhausts because of the vegetable oil which was then used.

It is not only in the refinement of oil that lubrication and fuelling of racing cars has become an exact science. If a car carries too much fuel it is carrying excess weight and is therefore handicapped against lighter opponents in just the same way as a racehorse is handicapped by an overweight jockey.

Benetton and all the others want to start a race with just the right amount of fuel. That means just enough to get the car over the finishing line. Sometimes in the history of the sport there have been horrible miscalculations (a classic example was Jack Brabham running out of fuel in sight of the finishing line in the 1970 British Grand Prix at Brands Hatch and desperately, and vainly, trying to push his car over the line before Jochen Rindt could overtake him). Nowadays the fuel experts calculate how much fuel is required using scientific data. Even so, there are still clangers from time to time.

In the case of Benetton, the Mobil experts start with a calculation based upon the known requirements of the Ford engine and the race distance, the latter normally not varying very much. Nevertheless, the nature of some circuits means that they are more 'thirsty' than others and for these circuits the Mobil boys will reshuffle the ingredients of the fuel in order to provide a heavier, more dense mixture offering a higher energy content within a specific volume.

During the season, the Mobil experts will also carry out random checks on their own fuel to check the octane level. The maximum per-

Testing by Brabham technicians in the pit road at Brands Hatch.

Sometimes the driver can't help feeling neglected.

Final check before going out on a testing session at Brands.

mitted octane rating in Formula 1 racing is 102 RON and if this limit is exceeded driver and car may be disqualified and the team fined. A small tolerance is allowed by the authorities but the tendency today is for the fuel manufacturers to refine their products to a slightly lower octane level. The reason for this is that octane tests sometimes vary from laboratory to laboratory and also the tests are done on a single cylinder rig whereas the fuel is, of course, intended to be used in a multi-cylinder engine. (In 1988, fuel which had passed Mobil and other tests was deemed by the authorities to be 0.1 octane over the permitted limit and a furore resulted.)

By refining fuel to a slightly lower octane limit there is less risk of trouble resulting from variations in lab tests. Nor does a minute reduction in octane rating cause any detectable variation in performance, according to Mobil.

Success comes down to hard facts rather than theories. When the engine and chassis manufacturers and designers, the tyre manufacturers and oil companies, the 'back-room' scientists in

their laboratories and the sponsors and other 'money-men' have all had their say, at the end of the day the majority of races, in the final analysis, are still won and lost not only by the skills and mistakes of drivers (naturally) but also by just how well the mechanics do their job.

A loose connection . . . a wheel-change seconds longer than that of a rival . . . a mistake in the heat of the moment . . . these errors can bring a multi-million pound project mournfully down to earth. And when everything goes right and the car and the driver do their stuff, the mechanics are not the ones to get the lion's share of the glory – or the cash. Yet race mechanics remain a special breed, hard-working, loyal, unsung heroes, often with a wry sense of humour.

Anyone who wants to get inside the skin of one of these unique gentlemen should beg, borrow or steal a copy of *Alf Francis – Racing Mechanic*. Written more years ago than he probably cares to remember by Peter Lewis it is not far short of the best book ever written on motor-racing and is certainly the best ever written about race mechanics. (It was published a long time ago, hence the advice to beg, borrow or steal although rare motor-book seller Eoin Young might have a copy for sale.)

Peter virtually lived for a season with Alf Francis (whose real name was something unpronounceable except in Polish) and everything comes across. Mostly the problems, of course, but also the man, in good mood and foul, in failure and success. One is left with the overall impression that, just as in war it's a good thing to have a battalion of Gurkhas by your side, in motor-racing you can't go wrong (at least not too far wrong) with a dozen Alf Francises. And in motor-racing there are still today many mechanics cast in the Francis mould.

This tradition is, perhaps, exemplified by Benetton mechanic, Pat Fry, in writing about his assignment during testing – logging all the data and then passing it on to the engineers to assist them in finding a good set-up for the car.

'To turn the black art into science you need a vast amount of performance data – load levels, airflows, coolant flows, aerodynamic pressures, steer inputs, brake pressures, wheel speeds and so on. All are gathered and collated into known operating parameters of the car.

'It's an uphill struggle against adverse temperatures, immense vibration and "G" loadings and one's ability to remember everything during the very short time available to alter the data logger set up during the test session.

'Everyone has an off day now and again but when I have a "drop off", part of the data logging system (affectionately known to the team as the "Logging Boll**ks") ends up dangling from the back of the car, retained only by an electrical cable or two. So going flat out down the start/finish straight at Imola followed closely by an entire data logging system which was gradually being reeled in as the wires wrapped themselves around the driveshafts.

'Having only been in this business for a very short time compared to some of the

mechanics on the team, one soon becomes aware of the famous (or should it be infamous?) "I told you so" Club, the founder member of which should, for the sake of my orthodontist, remain nameless. "The thermocouple's broken" . . . I told you so. "This wire has been crushed" . . . I told you so. "That box is loose" . . , I told you so. "Ha, ha this has melted" . . . you've guessed it. And then there's the standard cry as one approaches the car with a new item of test equipment: "Jesus. Do you know what that is going to weigh at the end of Hangar Straight?"

'But at least there is plenty of assistance in fitting the kit to the car – and it comes in many forms. For instance, wrapping copious quantities of heat shield over the laser ride height sensor so that it can't see the ground, or removing bits of bodywork without first removing the electrical connections.

'After working all day we do have a good laugh come the evening. You may be surprised that one needs to be careful of black ice in Estoril town centre in the middle of August – especially at about four o'clock in the morning. It is believed that the black ice was the cause of a number of test-team personnel falling over on the way back to the hotel from a disco.

'Also a problem is the Doberman dog that chased me around the swimming-pool when we did finally get back to the hotel – believe me, that's the last thing that you need at four in the morning.

'Pembrey, oh Pembrey. Everyone should really visit the charming little residence that we stay in when testing at this circuit in southern Wales. The Old Moat House, right outside Kidwelly Castle, is a thirteenth-century building full of character – oak beams, a large open fireplace, expensive antiques and the "incredible foldaway shower", which really must be seen to be believed.

'On our second trip there we came prepared with cameras and flash guns and headed straight for this contraption. Our esteemed leader climbed in wearing his clothes and we prepared

Mechanics can have a trying time. The Cooper crew discuss a problem with boss John Cooper (in the car) before international class record attempts.

to take the photographs. At this point the hotel owner walks in, doesn't seem at all concerned and, in fact, tries to turn the shower on with our leader still aboard.'

Pat's thoughts give some idea of the humour and camaraderie which exists among the race mechanics of today just as it did amongst those of yester-year (although some of the old-timers might be appalled at the contrivances involved in data logging).

One can't fail but to be impressed by the manner in which mechanics get on with the job and, whatever happens and however much they may curse and swear, keep at the task until the

Not all the dangers of motor-racing are on the circuit. A certain Benetton mechanic, taking time off for a round of golf, slipped down a rabbit-hole – and broke his leg. Team manager's comments duly censored . . .

job is done. First impressions are often the best; my first impression of the breed was soon after the Second World War when Fred Sowery, driving a Cooper, broke a number of international class records with the assistance of jovial John Cooper and his boys.

Those Cooper mechanics had a trying time. Hanging around because the Swiss timing equipment was held up by over-officious Customs, problems with the engine, problems with the tyres (all worsened by the shortages occasioned by war), working on the car to get it right and then finding the local pub closed at two o'clock and there was nowhere else to get a sandwich or a cup of coffee and so on and so on.

Yet they kept at it until those records were broken and there was hardly an imprecation (well, maybe two or three) amongst the lot.

Benetton's mechanics have, over the years, been generally of the same sterling mould. It is an area where the Witney team would seem to have little to worry about.

CHAPTER 5

The Drivers: Travelling in Hope

'Men are being paid almost half a million dollars just to line up for the start of a Grand Prix,' gasped a Sunday newspaper correspondent at the dawn of the 1990s. That was not the case when Toleman took their first tentative steps into Grand Prix racing at the beginning of the 1980s – and even if there were drivers collecting that sort of money they would not have been in the Toleman team who were working on a shoestring by Grand Prix standards.

In a mixed bag of three Italians, two Englishmen, a Swede, a Brazilian and a Venezuelan there was, however, one at least who would turn out to be a champion.

Prophets, they say, are without honour in their own country. That most certainly is not true of the Brazilian, Ayrton Senna. He may be criticized by colleagues, quarrel with his teammates and be disliked by a section of the public but in his own country he is a king, honoured by the Government and revered by his fellow countrymen. In 1989, Brazil issued a postage stamp commemorating Senna's World Championship and featuring a close-up of the driver wearing his helmet. Those buying a sheet of stamps had the bonus of reproductions of the McLaren car in the margins.

Even in Europe Senna may have more supporters than a perusal of the public prints might indicate. After the gritty exchanges of the 1989 season he was attacked on many fronts but these served only to generate a lively correspondence in the motor-sport journals – and many of those letters were from people who regarded Senna as the next best thing to sliced bread.

All this controversy was way ahead when the solemn-faced young South American joined Toleman in 1984. He had the label of champion on him from the early days. He himself says he wanted to be champion since he was four years old. Which is probably true since his father, a wealthy businessman, bought him a purpose-built, single-horsepower kart before he went to school. Senna, born Ayrton Senna da Silva (Senna is his mother's maiden name) in Sao Paulo on 21 March 1960, was hooked from the moment the kart was unloaded in front of the house and he was tucked into the driving seat. Car racing became his obsession and his family supported him all the way.

He was allowed to abandon his studies and the opportunity of running the family business in order to concentrate solely on his driving. In 1979 he was runner-up in the World Karting Championship and again in 1980, having been the South American Champion in 1977 and 1978. He came to Europe, more specifically to England, in 1981 and became British Formula Ford Champion. He was a popular figure at Snetterton, that great nursery of race drivers, and even today the official Ayrton Senna Fan Club has its headquarters at the Norfolk circuit.

To the impatient Senna, the Formula Ford Championship was not the instant passport to success that he had hoped for. No wealthy sponsors rushed forward and he went home to Brazil to water-ski, to help in the family business – and to talk about retiring from racing at the age of 21!

Motor-racing won. The diversions of Sao Paulo both at work and play could not disguise

The Ralt cars in which Ayrton Senna cut his eye-teeth and which formed the basis of many Toleman successes in Formula 2.

the fact that for once in his life Senna had no racing to look forward to, no commitment to a sport which had been a major part of his life for something like seventeen years. He raised some money, returned to England and had a highly successful season racing Formula Ford 2000 and winning the European Championship. He switched to Formula 3 in 1983 and, driving a Ralt-Toyota, became British champion.

Toleman signed Senna to a three-year contract and in 1984 the Brazilian made a formidable début in Grand Prix racing with a second and two third places. His other high places were one sixth and two sevenths and he was ninth in the struggle for the Drivers' Championship, undoubtedly a man to watch. His best perfor-

mance was in a controversial race at Monaco which started in the rain and was then stopped on lap 31 when Senna was running second. In the British Grand Prix at Brands Hatch and in the final race of the season, the Portuguese Grand Prix, he was third.

The controversy which has never been far away throughout his career was abundant in his first (and only) season for Toleman. He was involved in accidents in Montreal, Detroit and at the Nürburgring and, his critics said, was lucky to finish at Monaco after clouting the kerb and taking off. Ayrton criticized the officials (there would be other such occasions) saying that if it was too dangerous to continue at Monaco it must have been too dangerous to start.

Before the British Grand Prix, Senna went on record as saying Toleman were a good team with a very good car and he would be happy to stay with them for a long time. He finished third, retired in the German, Austrian and Dutch Grands Prix and then, after an internal dispute, was suspended from the team and missed the Italian Grand Prix. He came back for the Nürburgring and Estoril but his contract had a 'buy out' clause. Senna took advantage of it to join front-running Lotus team. 'A long time' had turned out to be to the end of the season.

His first Grand Prix victory, in Portugal, soon came and, in 1988, he joined McLaren and won the World Championship. He is generally agreed to be the fastest man on the circuits, with the possible exception of the British driver, Nigel Mansell, but always there has been criticism. Mansell, himself no stranger to slings and arrows, described him as 'a total idiot' (Senna, after one race, said of Mansell, 'He could have killed me'). The Italian Michele Alboreto, said Senna was a 'madman'; his McLaren rival Alain Prost summed up, 'The problem with Ayrton is that he cannot accept not winning.'

Controversy has never been far away from Ayrton Senna. In 1984, Toleman considered suing him. Senna, driving for Toleman, and with five rounds of the 1984 Championship still to go, signed for Lotus and apparently agreed that the announcement should be made before the Dutch Grand Prix. Toleman were understandably miffed. Senna's contract with them had a comparatively cheap 'buy out' clause but what angered them was the manner in which the affair had been handled. 'Depending on whether or not our lawyers believe it to be correct, we are quite prepared *not* to run Senna in the remaining races,' said Team Director Alex Hawkridge, 'I mean you can't very well employ a man you are suing for damages.'

In the sequel, Toleman suspended Senna for one race but he then finished out the season.

Just another bizarre episode in the strange odyssey of Ayrton Senna.

Jackie Stewart, three times World Champion, gave his opinion during the 1989 season that Senna still made too many mistakes and misjudgements to be considered a great driver. Certainly Senna has been involved in many incidents and accidents, not all of them his fault, and certainly he is obsessed with winning. Just as certain is that for one brief season a bright star twinkled across the Toleman firmament.

The two Englishmen who took Toleman into Grand Prix racing could hardly be more of a contrast to Senna. Brian Henton was one of a crop of very good British drivers in the 1960s and 1970s who had a few chances in the top flight but, perhaps because the car wasn't good enough or because there were other drivers who were better, never achieved world-beating status.

Henton was already in his thirtieth year before he made his Grand Prix début in a Lotus in 1975 and after winning the European Formula 2 Championship for Toleman he was a natural as No. 1 driver when Toleman moved into Formula 1.

The tale of that disheartening 1981 season has already been told but the man from Castle Donington did at least show that if the car stayed in one piece he could do his stuff by coming home tenth in the Italian Grand Prix at Monza.

Maybe that season was too much to bear. Henton and the Toleman team parted company and Henton drove for Arrows and Tyrrell in 1982. Henton was not exactly a household name but he was an outstanding Formula 2 driver and who knows what he might have achieved had he had a regular Grand Prix drive in the right car and at the right age? Certainly his contribution to the development of the Toleman team was a major one.

It was also somewhat of a surprise to the 'experts' who abound in motor-racing circles. The Toleman team was not at first taken too seriously, some regarding them as 'toys' for an extrovert successful businessman, Ted Toleman, and his co-director, Alex Hawkridge, who were

Nigel Mansell (shown) once called Ayrton Senna 'a total idiot'. Senna, after one race, alleged, 'Mansell might have killed me'.

just playing at a sport they liked. Towards the end of the 1978 season opinions began to change and when they teamed up with Jack Brabham's old partner, Ron Tauranac and his Ralt cars, whilst continuing their association with top-notch engine designer, Brian Hart, Toleman were obviously not to be lightly shrugged aside. Instead they looked a real threat to March and BMW, the twain dominating the Formula.

Eddie Cheever, the big American who drove for the Benetton-Alfa team in 1984.

There were a lot of good or promising drivers in Formula 2 at that time, including several who would be associated with the Toleman-Benetton story: Bruno Giacomelli, the reigning champion, Teo Fabi and Eddie Cheever.

Toleman's decision to go along with Brian Henton was the only weak link in the chain according to the 'experts'. The rugged motorbike dealer's personality might not fit into the Toleman set-up, they said – and they were proved wrong.

Henton had a couple of very good years with them in Formula 2 and followed with a season in Formula 1 before moving on. The only real controversy he was involved in arose from an on-the-track incident in the 1979 season. In the Enna race in Sicily there was a mêlée at the first corner and Henton took to the escape road, rejoining the race a few hundred yards further on – in the lead. After winning the race, the local stewards disqualified him, not for taking the escape road and coming out in front but for not stopping before rejoining the track and allegedly ignoring a marshal who was indicating that he should stop. (Which shows that there is nothing new under the sun. Or on the race circuit. Doesn't it, Nigel? Doesn't it, Ayrton?)

The Italian stewards upheld the Sicilians and so it became one of those minor *cause célèbre* with the Toleman team going to FISA to seek justice and the outcome not emerging until a couple of months after the season ended, by which time presumably many people had lost interest.

Incidentally, it is interesting to note that Henton's No. 2, Rad Dougall, who was to be succeeded by Derek Warwick in 1980, had a good season and was the winner at Thruxton when an accident insured that seven of the competitors never finished the first lap, Henton amongst them. Warwick, driving a March-Hart, was another.

Ironically, after leaving Toleman, Henton stepped into a seat with the Arrows team, vacated through injury to one of his closest rivals in Formula 2, the Swiss driver, Marc Surer. Team boss Jackie Oliver praised Henton's abilities as a test-driver. 'He has done a tremendous job for us,' he said.

However, Surer's recovery left no room for Henton in the team and so he moved to Tyrrell. Normally-aspirated cars were now having to fight turbos but Henton was in fifth place in the Swiss Grand Prix when his engine broke down. Thus Henton had to be content with a Formula 2 European Championship as memento of a long motor-racing career. Just another driver who was in the wrong car at the wrong place at the wrong time. Better drivers have achieved less. Worse drivers have accomplished more. It's the luck of the game it seems.

Toleman's other driver, Derek Warwick, stayed with the team for the 1982 season. He was some eight years younger than Henton, badly wanted to become an established Grand Prix driver and had signed a three-year contract with Toleman, just as Senna was to do later. Unlike Senna, Warwick saw the three years out, gaining valuable experience and improving all the while.

Born at Alresford in Hampshire on 28 August 1954, Warwick had also come up through Formula Ford and in 1976 was European Champion. After successfully partnering Henton in Formula 2 he moved with him into Grand Prix racing in 1981 but it was not until October of that year that he actually appeared in a race, the US Grand Prix at Las Vegas. This was a month after Henton had qualified for the Italian round.

It is very difficult to know where to put Derek Warwick in the Grand Prix scheme of things. The talent is there – Renault jumped at securing his services when the chance arose – but always something seems to have intervened every time he looked like shaping up as a championship contender. During those formative three years when he was with Toleman his results and those of the cars jointly improved – the two do not necessarily go together – as the record shows:

1981 Qualified one race. Retired.

1982 Qualified eleven races. Placed tenth and fifteenth. Retired nine.

1983 Qualified fifteen. Placed fourth (twice), fifth, sixth, seventh and eighth. Retired nine.

In several of the races in which he retired Warwick was well-placed at the time, notably at Monaco where he was lying fourth when he and Marc Surer collided on lap 50. Derek moved on to Renault and to Arrows but despite numerous fine drives a second place was the best he had achieved in 100 Grand Prix appearances up to 1989.

In so many ways, Warwick's career has paralleled that of Senna. The encouragement of his father from an early age, although in Warwick's case his father had been a racer himself, and then into kart racing. Senna started at four, Warwick at twelve. Then, unusually for those aspiring to motor-racing fame, Derek moved into stock car racing and at the age of 19 was Super Stock World Champion.

When he did decide to go into motor-racing proper he did wonders in Formula Ford (33 wins in 62 starts in 1976) and battled with world-champ-to-be Nelson Piquet, for the Formula 3 title throughout 1978 ending the season as Vandervell Formula 3 champion. Formula 2 in 1979 as a private entrant was a failure but then he joined the Toleman Formula 2 team and finished runner-up to team-mate Brian Henton in the 1980 European Championship.

So why has Senna achieved the very top and Warwick still struggles? It could be the cars. Just as a jockey can't go without the horse so a race driver can't win without the right car. It may be the mental outlook. Senna, so they say, believes that God goes with him. Moreover, he has a single-minded obsession with racing and winning. His short-lived marriage did not survive his intense devotion to motor-racing. On the other hand it is difficult to imagine Warwick, a happy family man, putting motor-racing before his wife and children.

At work on Nannini's car at the 1989 Spanish Grand Prix.

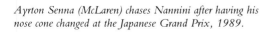

Ayrton Senna (McLaren) chases Nannini after having his nose cone changed at the Japanese Grand Prix, 1989.

(Right)   *Alessandro Nannini in a cheerful mood.*

(Below)   *Emmanuele Pirro follows the direction arrows in the 1989 Japanese Grand Prix. They didn't help – he had an accident on lap 33.*

(Above)   *A shot of Nannini in action during the 1989 Australian Grand Prix.*

(Left)   *Thierry Boutsen relaxes in Australia.*

(Above)   *Johnny Herbert – in the happy half of the season for him.*

(Right)   *Emmanuele Pirro: the man in disguise.*

(Above) *Johnny Herbert in action during the 1989 American Grand Prix.*

(Left) *Nannini at Estoril for the 1989 Portuguese Grand Prix.*

Follow my leader: Pirro (Benetton) tailed by Ivan Capelli
(March) and Andreas de Cesaris (BMS Dallara) during the
Portuguese Grand Prix.

Prost (McLaren) and Nannini (Benetton) fight it out during
the 1989 British Grand Prix.

Nannini and Boutsen during the French Grand Prix in 1989.

Inside the Benetton garage at the Canadian Grand Prix.

*Traffic engineering: Ivan Capelli (March), René Arnoux (Ligier), Nelson Piquet (Lotus),
Riccardo Patrese (Williams) and Johnny Herbert (Benetton) at Monaco.*

Herbert, de Cesaris and Boutsen in the San Marino Grand Prix.

Teo Fabi, the Italian who drove for the Witney team under both the Toleman and the Benetton banners.

Close-up of Boutsen in the 1987 British Grand Prix.

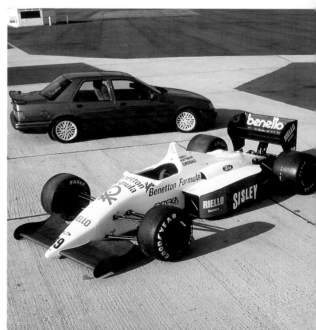

The Benetton colour scheme was somewhat different in 1987.

Boutsen and Fabi who did well together in the 1987 Benetton team.

(Right) *Boutsen leading the 1988 Canadian Grand Prix from his team-mate Nannini and Nelson Piquet (Lotus). The Belgian would win the race the following year – driving for Williams.*

(Below) *Plenty of tools – and plenty of spares – required at every race. The Benetton mechanics at work.*

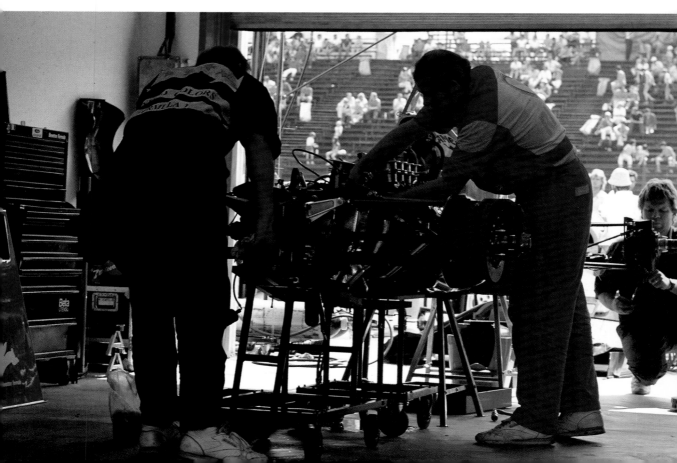

(Above)   *Mansell was again in the headlines in 1990; here he is driving for Williams and chasing the Benetton of Nannini in the 1988 French Grand Prix.*

(Left)   *Piquet suited up in his livery and looking happy about it.*

(Above)   *Nelson Piquet tyre-testing at Estoril, December 1989.*

(Right)   *Alessandro Nannini at the British Grand Prix.*

Piquet in the pits at Estoril.

Alessandro Nannini: the man to take Benetton to the top? At the Spanish Grand Prix (above)
and racing in Brazil (below).

As Warwick approaches the veteran stage, the 1990s will show if a world title is still within his grasp.

Most of the other drivers in the Witney stable in pre-Benetton days, Senna and Warwick apart, were of the group of Formula 2 drivers who pick up regular rides without ever threatening to become winners. Unluckiest of them was Johnny Cecotto, Warwick's team partner in 1984. Johnny was that rarity in European motor-racing, a Venezuelan (he was born there on 25 January 1956) but like many other car racers – Surtees, Nuvolari, Taruffi, Hailwood, and so on – he had been a top motorbike rider before switching to four wheels.

Based in Italy, Cecotto had been World 350cc Champion in 1975 and 750cc Champion in 1978. When he switched to cars he was runner-up for the 1982 Formula 2 European Championship and made his Grand Prix début with the Theodore team in Brazil in 1983, moving to Toleman the following year.

The triumphs he had achieved on two wheels eluded him on four; a ninth place in the Canadian Grand Prix and an unclassified finish in the San Marino Grand Prix at Imola were the nearest he came to glory. He spun off at Monaco, hit the wall in Dallas and his practice accident at Brands Hatch put him out for the season and virtually ended his career.

The man who took Cecotto's seat in the Toleman team for the last three races of the 1984 season is one of Grand Prix racing's mysteries. A Swede, Stefan Johansson was born on 8 September 1956. He spent a lot of his time in London and was British Formula 3 Champion in 1980, though since then his career has taken some puzzling turns. There are drivers who have hung in there for sixty or seventy races without scoring more than a point or two. Johansson, after 70 races had 80 points and yet he has never seemed to settle with one team or emerge as a serious contender for honours.

The year he won the Formula 3 title Johansson also made his Grand Prix début, driving and failing to qualify a Shadow in Argentina and Brazil. In 1981 and 1982 he drove in Formula 2 with a private Toleman and then a Spirit-Honda, but in 1983 he drove a limited programme of Grand Prix races with the Spirit-Honda turbo, reputedly a very difficult car to drive. In 1984 he 'substituted' at Tyrrell before taking over Cecotto's seat at Toleman.

He did quite well. Fourth in the Italian Grand Prix, he retired from the European Grand Prix at the Nürburgring with overheating problems when he was in twelfth place; in the last race of the season, at Estoril, he was eleventh.

It was good enough, anyway, for Toleman to sign Johansson for the following season. Unfortunately, however, owing to lack of a tyre supplier, Toleman had to miss the first three races and so when Johansson had the chance to join Ferrari in April, Toleman released him. The Ferrari period represents the peak of his Grand Prix years but Johansson did not stay put and kept adding to his collection of good and bad cars. In 1989 he was No. 1 driver for Onyx, the English-based team managed by Mike Earle.

If Johansson's motor-racing career is a bit of a mystery what does one make of Piercarlo Ghinzani, who replaced him in the 1985 Toleman team after the Swede had moved to Ferrari? Piercarlo is one of those who have had a lot of Grand Prix drives without ever achieving anything much. Indeed, as the 1989 season loomed, he had one scoring finish, a fifth place, to show in seventy-one starts. He was the 1977 European Formula 3 Champion and 1976 Italian Champion but has never been near winning form in Formula 1. He made his Grand Prix début in 1981 with Osella and has spent most of his time with them. In seven starts with Toleman he didn't finish a race and in one of them stalled at the start and never got going. Mark you, Grand Prix racing has rarely been his No. 1 priority, unlike the majority of drivers today. Piercarlo has spent much of his time building up a flourishing Lancia agency. And there are many, including his great friend, Michele Alboreto, who will say that Piercarlo's record

John Surtees seen here with Count Agusta, of MV Agusta fame.

Johnny Cecotto was not as lucky on four wheels as Tazio Nuvolari, seen here in an Auto Union at Donington Park before the war . . .

would be greatly different had he ever had a good car – the man really can drive, they say.

His career poses the question: are there no other drivers who deserve a chance? A year or two away from 40, Ghinzani is hardly likely to improve. But then, in fairness, top-class drivers are hardly likely to jump at the chance of driving an Osella since the Italian cars have rarely looked like scoring points, let alone winning, in eleven years of Formula 1.

Two Italian drivers who made a more major contribution, at least to the Toleman team, are the remaining two of the pre-Benetton period, Teo Fabi and Bruno Giacomelli.

Giacomelli had just the one season, 1983, but managed sixth, seventh, eighth and ninth places in fourteen starts. He was already a fairly experi-

enced Grand Prix driver when he joined the Witney team. Born on 10 September 1952, he was European Formula 2 Champion in 1978, made his Grand Prix début with McLaren in Italy the previous year and drove five times for the same team during 1978. He was with Alfa Romeo from 1979 until joining Toleman.

If there were such things, Teo Fabi would almost qualify for a long-service medal from Witney. He was with Toleman in 1982 and rejoined the team in 1985 just as Benetton became associated with the Toleman set-up. He remained with Benetton for the following two seasons, 1986 and 1987. History may record that Fabi was a better driver than the statistics show. The Milanese (he was born there on 9 March 1955) raced karts, Formula Ford and

99

Formula 3 in Italy before joining the March Formula 2 team in 1981. Although he was beaten out for the European Championship by the British driver Geoff Lees (Ralt-Honda), Fabi had attracted the attention of Toleman and made his Grand Prix début for them in 1982.

Failures to qualify, retirements and one unclassified finish did not strike him as a particularly triumphant venture into Grand Prix circles and so he accepted invitations to race in the US the following year where his initial venture into CANAM had impressed. It was here that Fabi's true ability showed. At the Indianapolis 500 he qualified his March-Cosworth in pole position at an average speed of 207.39mph (333.76kph) for four laps, a record for Indy. In the CART Championship he was a close second to the great American driver, Al Unser Senr. In 1984 he attempted the virtually impossible. Loth to forego the US where he had already achieved much, he was still keen on making the grade in Formula 1 and signed for the Brabham team with the intention of combining Grand Prix racing and the CART Championship, a heavy burden in travelling time.

It was a difficult situation. Fabi had already signed American contracts when the Brabham chance came along. Brabham needed a partner for Piquet. Piquet was not keen on it being Senna but preferred another Brazilian, Roberto Moreno. Bernie Ecclestone, the team's owner, was not too keen on Moreno. Parmalat, the Italian sponsors of the team, preferred an Italian. Hence Fabi. There could be clashes of dates but apparently everyone was happy with the thought that Teo's younger brother Corrado might be able to deputize if necessary. Corrado was the 1982 European Formula 2 Champion and made his Grand Prix début in 1983 with the Osella team. In the sequel, Corrado did deputize for his brother in a couple of races, Teo picked up points in some of the others and both missed the last race of the season owing to the death of their father.

Teo had already decided to give up the US

and to concentrate on Grands Prix until taking over the family business in about three years time. Now his father's death clouded the situation. Brabham did not renew his contract and so, in 1985, shortly before the Monaco Grand Prix, Fabi found himself back at Witney with Ghinzani in the second car. It was a holding year in many respects, three races missed through lack of tyres, reorganization of the team and the Benetton interest so Fabi's twelfth place, the best either driver could manage, did not matter much one way or the other.

Teo was back again in 1986 (this time with Gerhard Berger) and so became the only driver to straddle the Witney period driving both for Toleman and for Benetton. He had two full seasons with Benetton, first with the BMW engine and then with the Ford-Cosworth turbo, finishing in the top ten five times in 1986 and seven times the following year, his best performance being third in the Austrian Grand Prix.

There was another Toleman driver during this period – and very few people would be able

Ayrton Senna, the man Gordon Message says is the best driver ever to race from the Witney stable.

to give the correct answer at a motor-racing quiz if asked: Who was he?

The answer is: Pierluigi Martini.

This is the strange story behind it. Martini was born at Lavezzola, Italy, on 23 April 1961. He had an uncle, Giancarlo Martini, who had raced internationally without ever making the Grand Prix grade, although he had once driven at Brands Hatch in a non-championship race in a Ferrari loaned to him by the works. The young Pierluigi naturally regarded his uncle as a hero and through him became more and more immersed in motor-sport.

Driving as soon as he was old enough, Pierluigi made a good start in racing in 1980, competing in four Formula Italia events before moving straight into Formula 3. He continued to progress and in 1983 became European Formula 3 Champion. He also had a Formula 2 outing at Misano where he finished second. He had his heart set on Grand Prix racing and as European Champion hoped he might make a direct transition from Formula 3 to Formula 1. There was a place going in the Brabham team at the time and it was on this that Martini's hopes were centred.

It was not to be. Teo Fabi got the vacant seat and a disappointed Pierluigi decided to accept an offer of a regular drive with the Martini Lancia endurance racing team, the Martinis in question, of alcoholic fame, being no relation to him.

However, when the Italian Grand Prix came round in October of that year, 1984, an unexpected chance came up. Ayrton Senna, who had been driving well for Toleman, was disciplined by his team and suspended from the Italian race. So Toleman had two cars and one driver – the Swede Johansson who had taken over from the injured Johnny Cecotto.

Martini was given a crack at the second car. Alas, there was no fairy tale ending. He failed to qualify. However, his Grand Prix chance had not gone. Nannini, who would later become Benetton's No. 1 driver, failed to get the necessary Super-licence for Grand Prix racing in 1985 and the seat he was scheduled to fill in the Minardi team became vacant. Martini got it.

He had a pretty disastrous first year, rehabilitated himself in Formula 3000 and showed signs of being very quick indeed. He even got in the scoring points, something which doesn't happen too often to the 'minnows' of Grand Prix racing.

Senna was the most brilliant of the Toleman drivers, Cecotto the unluckiest, Fabi perhaps the most consistent but the team probably owes most to the two Englishmen who kept plugging away in the darkest days . . . Henton and Warwick. Not to mention the mechanics and other backroom boys and girls who worked tirelessly to send out cars which, for a long time, were non-competitive, always in the hope and faith that their luck would change.

CHAPTER 6

The Drivers: 'The Four Horsemen'

Four drivers 'worked' for Benetton in the seasons before the Italian concern moved into team ownership. One sped but briefly across the Grand Prix scene but the other three are still driving in the 1990s and one of them, probably the best of them, gave Benetton their first victory.

Michele Alboreto, an Italian, born in Milan on 23 December 1956, is a driver whose career has touched upon greatness without ever quite achieving it. Some future motor-racing historian, trying to evaluate the comparative worth of Grand Prix drivers in the latter half of the twentieth century will probably put Alboreto high in the Second Division. Results alone must put him behind Piquet, Prost, Senna and Mansell but Alboreto is way, way out in front of many other experienced drivers and at least he enters his veteran years with five Grand Prix victories to his credit.

He stepped straight from Formula 3 – he was European Champion in 1980 – into Grand Prix racing where he made his début in 1981 with the Tyrrell team. He won his first Grand Prix at Las Vegas in 1982 and was with Tyrrell when Benetton sponsored the Surrey-based equipe in 1983. His win at Detroit gave a shot in the arm to a new sponsor just at the right time although it did not prevent team and sponsor coming to a parting of the ways at the end of the season.

Alboreto kept up his win-a-year gait with the Belgian Grand Prix in 1984 but his subsequent career has not always fulfilled the very obvious talent of the man. Perhaps the most disappointing years were in the late 1980s when the dream of a top Italian driver piloting the top Italian car – Ferrari – to the World Championship, failed to materialize.

It had started well. When Alboreto joined 'The Prancing Horse' in April 1984, he became the first Italian-born driver with the team since Arturo Merzario in 1973. In his first year he became the first Italian to win a Grand Prix with Ferrari since Scarfiotti had won at Monza in 1966. Hopes were high but the dreams of a world title for 1984 remained just dreams. Not that it could be laid entirely at Alboreto's door. . .

By this time he was much improved over the driver who, in his earlier years, was sometimes criticized by fellow-drivers for a certain lack of 'track etiquette', which may come as a surprise to those who think that Ayrton Senna 'invented' this style of driving.

The Ulster-born driver, John Watson, a very good driver himself, and veteran of more than 150 Grands Prix (many think his Formula 1 career was curtailed far too early), described Alboreto as 'arguably the best Italian driver around at this time.' He *must* have been good for Enzo Ferrari to hire him. It was said that for an Italian to be considered for Italy's greatest racing team he had to be exceptionally good, the venerable Enzo applying harsher assessments to his fellow countrymen than to drivers of other nationalities.

Alboreto returned to Tyrrell for the 1989 season but, perhaps surprisingly in view of his earlier association, failed to settle in happily and by mid-season was announcing his disenchant-

John Watson (shown), veteran of more than 150 Grand Prix races, reckoned Michele Alboreto 'arguably the best Italian driver around'.

ment and letting it be known that he would welcome a switch to another team. 'I don't want to continue with Tyrrell but I don't want to break my contract either.' When the situation emerged in the public prints, Benetton-Ford (seeking a replacement for Johnny Herbert) and Lola both expressed interest. There were suggestions that Benetton had tried to get Alboreto earlier – the team was under a great deal of pressure from the aggressive Italian press who collectively seemed to require that Benetton should use Italian drivers exclusively. (A member of the aggressive Italian press once punched Alboreto on the nose!) In the sequel, Michele ended up with Lola-Lamborghini but not for long.

Jackie Oliver, former racing-driver who headed the Arrows team, signed the Milanese for the 1990 season which meant, that Arrows, a team which often threatened to deliver but never quite made it, would for the first time have a regular driver who had actually *won* a Grand Prix! If there is such a thing as security in motor-racing then the Arrows set-up, in Grand Prix racing for some eleven-plus years and with expansion already planned for its new Milton Keynes factory, comes very near to it.

Certainly to the 33-year-old Italian it obviously seemed a better proposition than Lola where the Lamborghini engine had not yet given consistent reliability although undoubtedly fast. The Lola team had also been without the presence of a backer since the last to hold that status had been arrested.

103

Alboreto's arrival at Milton Keynes saw the departure of two other former Benetton-linked drivers, Derek Warwick and the American, Eddie Cheever.

Cheever drove for Benetton in 1984 when they switched from sponsoring Tyrrell to Alfa Romeo. Although taking part in more than 130 Grands Prix, the big fellow, born 1 January 1958, had, like Warwick, only a second place to show as his best finish but in all fairness he had rarely had a car worthy of his ability. Then as the cars got smaller, big Ed got more uncomfortable and it became highly problematic if he was to be seen much more in Grands Prix. Determination and talent are all very well but they don't win races on their own. Cheever did fairly well by Benetton during their brief sponsorship of Alfa. His partner was another middling good driver, the Italian Riccardo Patrese, and both would have done well with less thirsty and more reliable engines.

Eddie Cheever is a very Europeanised (if there is such a term) American, rather like the dashing race driver of an earlier era, the Franco–American Harry Schell. Although born in Phoenix, Arizona, Cheever's father put the usual Italy–USA emigration flow into reverse by moving to Rome. There Eddie grew up and, like so many race drivers of today, started kart racing, in his case, at the age of twelve. He was the leading driver of the Italian kart team which won the 1973 European Championship and was runner-up in the 1974 World Championship.

Though barely old enough to have a driving licence, Eddie started racing Formula Ford and Formula 3 cars in England. He was only 20 when he had his first Formula 1 drives with Hesketh and Theodore but, with cars and driver untried, the ventures were not successful. Instead, Eddie concentrated on Formula 2 and was fourth in the European Championship in 1979 with Osella. He returned to Formula 1 with the Osella team in 1980 and then in rapid succession drove for Tyrrell, Ligier, Renault and Alfa Romeo. His best season was with

Renault in 1983 – sixth in the World Championship. He also raced with the Lancia team in endurance events.

However, it is not without significance that Cheever's best Grand Prix season was with a team doing well at the time – Renault – and a good car. In 1989, he had a slight consolation, finishing third in his hometown Grand Prix at Phoenix.

Riccardo Patrese, born in Padova, Italy, on 17 April 1954, went into the motor-racing record books in 1989 by becoming the man with more Grand Prix starts than any other driver in history. Yet, as he approached his 200th race he had only two wins to show for that record – Monaco in 1982 and South Africa in 1983.

Of course, he has driven a variety of cars during his career and not all of them, by a long way, have been serious contenders. They include Shadow, Arrows, Brabham, Alfa Romeo and Williams. Yet another European Formula 3 champion, 1976 being his year, Patrese's best racing season was probably in 1982 when, in addition to winning his first Grand Prix, he was also runner-up in the World Sports Car Championship.

So many races, so much experience – perhaps a certain degree of the erratic in his driving accounts for the small number of victories? Here is what some of the critics have said of him over the years:

'Qualifies better than he races.'
'Quick but not consistently so.'
'Career uncertain – like his driving.'

Be that as it may, Patrese certainly did his best to give Benetton value for money during the 1984 season he spent with them. It must also be remembered that he fought back after the trauma of 1978 when he was blamed by some drivers as being responsible for the fatal crash at Monza of the Swedish driver, Ronnie Peterson. He was later exonerated by an investigating tribunal.

Certainly Patrese enters the 1990s with a reputation as a much more level-headed and mature driver than he was in his salad days.

The fourth Benetton 'horseman' during the Tyrrell and Alfa seasons was an American, Danny Sullivan. There have been more Americans in modern Grand Prix racing than one might think at first – Dan Gurney, the tough Marine who was the son of an opera singer and who went on to build his own cars; Mario Andretti, the Italian-born driver who was great at Indy and great on the Grand Prix circuits; Richie Ginther and, of course, Eddie Cheever, but some Americans have appeared but briefly.

One such was Sullivan, he of the good fighting name. Born on 9 March 1950, Danny was

(Right) *Patrese, who drove for Benetton in 1984, had fought back after being blamed by some for the death of Sweden's Ronnie Peterson (shown) at Monza. A tribunal exonerated him.*

Dan Gurney in a parade of drivers at Brands Hatch – the ex-Marine son of an opera singer was one of the handful of Americans to become a top Grand Prix driver.

already approaching the veteran stakes when he joined Alboreto in the 1983 Benetton–Tyrrell team. Hailing from Louisville, Kentucky, home of the 'Big Lip' (Cassius Clay, later Muhammed Ali), Danny had been third in the 1982 CANAM Championship before crossing the Atlantic to try his luck in Formula 1. It was a nostalgic journey for Danny because he had been 'weaned' on motor-racing at the Snetterton 'academy for fast young gentlemen' run by headmaster Jim Russell.

On his return to Europe, Sullivan may not have hit the headlines but he did put in some good performances including a sound fifth place at Monaco and second place in the non-championship Race of the Champions at Brands Hatch.

All in all, 'The Four Horsemen' didn't do badly by their sponsor – who was sufficiently encouraged to stay in motor-racing . . .

CHAPTER 7

The Drivers: The Benetton Boys

If Cecotto was one of the unluckiest of drivers, Gerhard Berger has to be the most fortunate although his good fortune – if that be the right term – came some time after his one-year sojourn with the Benetton team.

The Austrian, born 27 August 1959, was driving for Ferrari when it happened. On lap 4 of the 1989 San Marino Grand Prix, Senna, the eventual winner, Prost, Mansell and Patrese roared through Tamburello, a left-hand turn just after the pits. The next car, the blood-red Ferrari of Berger went straight on, hit the wall and ricocheted off, bouncing and scraping the barrier for two or three hundred yards, sparks and bits and pieces flying through the air. Then, as it juddered to a halt, minus a couple of wheels, the dreaded happened – it burst into flames.

Wonderful work by the marshals and the safe construction of the cockpit area of modern Grand Prix cars combined to save Berger. The first marshal aimed his extinguisher into the cockpit and the fire-fighting team had the blaze out in less than 24 seconds. Berger was conscious when he was brought back to the paddock and able to give the 'thumbs up' sign.

He suffered burns to his hands, arms and chest (around 15 per cent of his body according to the official bulletin) but nothing like severe enough to endanger his life. His other injuries were trifles bearing in mind he must have hit the barrier at around 170mph. He had a hairline fracture of his right shoulder-blade and a cracked rib – many a DIY man has suffered worse falling off a ladder while painting the kitchen. Berger was soon up and about again after an accident which just a few seasons before might well have been fatal.

Three years before this accident, Berger had had just one season with Benetton, when the B186 cars were powered with BMW engines. That season amply demonstrated the ability of the young Austrian. Teamed with Teo Fabi, the little man of few words, Berger put in some impressive performances. In nearly every race he did *not* finish he was in the top six or top ten when he retired. And in those he did finish he was in the top six five times, in the top ten eight times.

He was third at Imola where he was to crash so disastrously three years later but his best performance by far was in Mexico where he was a triumphant winner, joining Alboreto in the Benetton winners' Hall of Fame where later both would be joined by 'Sandro' Nannini.

Berger is classified by friend and foe alike as a driver who always gives 100 per cent and his modest total of victories probably owes more to the domination of the Grand Prix scene by McLaren than to his own shortcomings. The fact that after his San Marino flamer he could be back in action for round 12 of the 1989 series, finishing second to Prost, indicates the calibre of the man. That he could then go on to Portugal and *win* was even better. Unfortunately, his well-earned victory was overshadowed by the Senna–Mansell crash and black flag arguments which obscured the fact that Berger qualified well, made a good start and was nursing a comfortable lead when Senna and Mansell disputed

The Belgian driver, Thierry Boutsen, who drove most consistently for the Benetton team.

the same piece of road. Berger showed that his comeback was no fluke when he added another second place, this time to Senna, in round 14 in Spain. To finish seventh in the World Drivers' Championship after such a bad accident was indeed a fine achievement by the Ferrari pilot, still young enough to be a top driver of the 1990s.

Like so many of his contemporaries, Berger started very young. He was still at school when he took part in his first Tyrolean hill-climb on a Kawasaki motorbike. Then, in a borrowed Ford Escort, he won his first car race. Subsequently he did well in the Alfasud European one-make series, Formula Ford 2000 and the German national Formula 3. Racing remained basically a hobby and he was seriously thinking of giving it up to concentrate all his energies on his trucking business when he was offerd help to continue in Formula 3. BMW came up with more help and that, in turn, led to Berger making his Formula 1 début with the ATS team in his native Austria, in August 1984.

ATS dropped out of racing at the end of that year and Berger broke his neck in a mid-winter road accident – his outlook was bleak. However, the resilient Austrian made a complete recovery from his injuries and took over Marc Surer's seat with the Arrows-BMW team in 1985.

When Benetton had switched from BMW to Ford, Fabi remained but Berger had gone, to be replaced by the Belgian driver, Thierry Boutsen. Although Boutsen's ambitions also originated in childhood – he learned to drive when he was eight and at twelve was racing motorbikes – his apprenticeship was rather longer than that of some of his contemporaries.

Born in Brussels on 17 July 1957, Boutsen eventually enrolled in the André Pilette driving school at Zolder and won the school's championship for Formula Vee single-seaters. That was the go-ahead signal the young Belgian wanted and the following year he was racing Formula Ford 1600 Hawke. To please his parents he had kept up his engineering studies and

now he found this knowledge invaluable when it came to setting up the car and tuning the engine. He now had to do his National Service but in spite of having to ask for permission before every race he won 15 out of 18 in 1978, driving a Crossle, and comfortably took the Benelux Formula Ford Championship, yet another of today's Grand Prix drivers who initially learned his trade through the ubiquitous Ford category.

During the next four years Boutsen would be runner-up in the European Formula 3 Championship; runner-up and third in the European Formula 2 Championship. It wasn't a smooth progression all the way. Although helped by his country's most famous driver, Jackie Ickx, Boutsen had a stuttering start in Formula 3 with a bad slump after winning first time out. A switch to the French-based Martini team did wonders for his results and his morale and began a love affair with the Nürburgring. In 1980 he won the opening round of the European Formula 3 battle on the 14-mile German circuit; in 1981 he won the equivalent Formula 2 race there in a March-BMW. The Ring, superb show-case for a driver's talents, gave Boutsen an opportunity he seized with delight.

Then, in 1982, he drove for the Spirit-Honda Formula 2 team, won three races and was ready for the big time. However, a slot in a Grand Prix team, especially one of the outfits outside 'the big league' often depends upon the amount of finance a driver can bring with him. Boutsen like Niki Lauda before him, had to take out a substantial bank loan in order to secure his first Formula 1 drive with the British-based Arrows. He made his début, appropriately enough, in the 1983 Belgian Grand Prix at Spa. And, again like Lauda, his investment in his own ability paid off.

As with a number of other teams, Arrows were hampered with a normally-aspirated engine at a time when the turbos were making their presence felt but, even so, the rookie driver finished seventh in both the Canadian

Boutsen with his new partner for the 1988 season, the Italian Alessandro Nannini.

and Detroit Grands Prix. He also hit the headlines in sports-car racing, winning the Monza 1000 KM in a Porsche with Bob Wollek as co-driver. Boutsen was undoubtedly quick and he stayed with Arrows for three years, his best results being second place in the 1985 San Marino Grand Prix at Imola.

Though 1986 was a very dismal year for both Arrows and Boutsen he again drove a Porsche to a sports-car win, this time on home ground at Spa. The following year he moved to Benetton. Teo Fabi was still there and now, between them, the two drivers did not have too bad a year. Boutsen himself was fifth in his first race in Brazil and third in the final race of the season,

the Australian Grand Prix. In between he picked up two fourth places, two fifth and – out of the scoring – a seventh and a fourteenth.

It was clear by now that Boutsen was one of those drivers who *must* win a Grand Prix one day. He was so near. In his second season with Benetton it seemed the day could not be long delayed but, alas, it was not to be although he strung together a remarkable sequence of results: 7, 4, 8, 8, 3, 3, retired, retired, 6, 3, 3, 6, 3, 9, 3, 5 – almost unbelievable consistency. But still no win. It is difficult not to believe that a victory would have come had he stayed with Benetton but instead he went to the crack Williams outfit in 1989 and broke the ice, not

At the British Grand Prix in 1989.

with one win but two, the Canadian and Australian Grands Prix.

Significantly, both races were affected by rain (an understatement in the case of Australia), an indication of the winning driver's quality. Boutsen's first Grand Prix win (in Canada) was, perhaps, more surprising than his second (although the Australian race had more of the ingredients of a novel). Everyone, but everyone, was expecting a McLaren-Honda walkover in the Canadian Grand Prix but the inclement weather evened the odds considerably.

Prost took an early lead in one McLaren, all according to the script. When he pulled out, team-mate Senna took over. Still according to script. Then, as the track started to dry out, drivers commenced pitting in order to swap wet weather tyres for slicks. Boutsen stopped on lap 11 but on lap 21, when Senna went in, Riccardo Patrese took on the lead. Lap 35 and Patrese went in to leave Derek Warwick in front but a couple of laps later Warwick dropped out and Senna was the leader again with Patrese second and Boutsen third. The Belgian gained steadily on Patrese and by lap 59 had reduced a 17 second gap to a narrow six-tenths of a second.

Finally, on lap 62, Boutsen got past Patrese and went after Senna. Five laps later the Brazilian's McLaren 'blew up' and Boutsen roared home for his first-ever World Championship win after so many near-misses. Certainly he had adequately demonstrated during his time with Benetton that he was well capable of such things.

Thierry Boutsen may be 'the one that got away', the driver whom Benetton will most miss. This decade will show . . . Meanwhile, any team which believes that talent runs in families might like to cast an eye over Thierry's wife, Patricia. She races karts and, during the supporting programme for the 1988 Belgian Grand Prix, she drove in the Alfa Romeo 164 Celebrity Race, coming second.

Nannini was Boutsen's partner in the latter's second season with Benetton and remained with the team through 1989 and 1990. He and other drivers associated with the team are, hopefully, Benetton's 'men of tomorrow'. Save one. Emanuele Pirro.

Pirro, born in Italy on 12 January 1962, had a Grand Prix record of ten races and a couple of points plus an established reputation as a test-driver when Benetton released him at the close of the 1989 season. Would he be back to Grand Prix racing? With some other team? Or even with Benetton? The competition is tough.

CHAPTER 8

The Drivers: Men of Tomorrow?

The Benetton Ford team stood at the crossroads as the 1990s began. During the next decade would it become a team to rank with the mighty McLaren, the legendary Ferrari and the brilliant Williams *equipes*? Or would it fade from the picture, just another of the Formula 1 ventures which never quite fulfilled its potential?

If the team was at the crossroads, so were some of the drivers, notably the pair with which Benetton began the campaign, Alessandro Nannini, of Italy, and Nelson Piquet, of Brazil; one, in crude terms, a 'never-waser', the other, just as harshly described, a 'has-been'.

There were many people who did not subscribe to either view. To take Nannini first . . .

The Italian won his first Grand Prix, the Japanese, in 1989 but was given little credit for it on account of the 'coming together' of teammates Senna and Prost and the subsequent disqualification of Senna. Yet Nannini drove well, kept a clear head and stayed away from trouble with Senna when another Prost situation threatened. The man does deserve some credit.

Most of his critics could not win a dodgem race let alone a Grand Prix. Yet, when it was announced that Piquet, a triple World Champion with 20 Grand Prix wins to his credit, was joining Nannini in the Benetton team, someone commented that the Italian would be just as fast as the ex-champion which said more about Piquet's decline, they opined, than Nannini's ability.

Despite a reputation for being 'slightly wild' 'Sandro' has improved all the while since join-

ing the Benetton team in 1988. At the end of his first season at Witney he was hailed by many as 'the find of the year'. Some of those who did so have since criticized him – presumably he let them down by failing to win the World Championship in quick order!

His route to Formula 1 was not the usual one of karting, Formula Ford and Formula 3. Most unusually, his first motor-sport event was in rallying and he started with, of all things, a Citroen Dyane, before switching to *the* rally car of the late 1970s, the Lancia Stratos, a world-beater in itself.

Born in Sienna (a town he still calls home) on 9 July 1959, Nannini was almost twenty-one when he won his first circuit race, driving a Formula Fiat Abarth single-seater in 1980. The following year he won the Italian National Championship. By-passing Formula 3, he went straight into Formula 2 with the small Italian firm of Minardi, founded by a Fiat dealer, Giancarlo Minardi, at Faenza in Northern Italy.

When Nannini joined the team, Minardi had been going for some ten years, first in Formula Italia, then Formula 3 and 2. After victory with a Ferrari engine in a Chevron chassis, Minardi asked Giacomo Caliri to design a Formula 2 car which proved successful in the hands of Michele Alboreto and others.

In the first race of the 1982 season, Nannini finished fifth at Silverstone and later in the season he was second at Misano, eventually being classified tenth in the European Championship. The last Formula 2 race on the Nürburgring in 1983 resulted in another second place but 1983

113

Nelson Piquet in a reflective mood: what does the next decade hold in store for the three-times World Champion as he joins forces with Benetton Ford?

and 1984 were not very happy years in terms of winning races, engine troubles causing his retirement many a time.

A brighter spot was at Le Mans where Sandro shared a Lancia with Le Mans specialist, Bob Wollek. They gained pole position and led the race until troubled by gearbox problems but the consolation for Nannini was that he set a new lap record before the problems began.

Meanwhile, Minardi had put Caliri to work on a Grand Prix car which was unveiled in 1984. Nannini expected to make his Grand Prix début the following season – in 1985 – but was floored when FISA refused to grant him the necessary Super-licence on the evidence of his Formula 2 results which, to be honest, were hardly exciting. However, after another season with Lancia he made his Formula 1 début in 1986.

It was a good training ground for a rookie driver. The little team had far from ample resources and it was always a struggle. (By 1989 the Minardis, now powered by Ford DFR, had improved to the extent of four places in the points during the season.)

Despite Sandro's lack of success with inadequate machinery, Benetton saw enough in his two seasons of trouble to make them think that here was a Grand Prix star of the future and they signed him for 1988 as No. 2 to the Belgian, Thierry Boutsen.

Boutsen, of course, had a very consistent season with ten finishes amongst the points and three more in the top nine but Nannini was something of a surprise with six scoring places and one more in the top nine. It showed what he was capable of with machinery which had a little more poke.

With Boutsen leaving the team, Nannini took over as No. 1 driver for 1989 – and his first Grand Prix victory. The years ahead should bring many more for the Italian. His team have no doubts about it. His ability to run at the front and finish regularly in the points merely confirmed what they knew already. They had been impressed by his natural flair and total commit-

ment (the two don't always go together) when he was with Minardi and his results in his first two seasons with Benetton confirmed that those first impressions had been right.

Now, for both driver and team, the World Driver's and Constructors' Championships are the goals and looking down the current list of Grand Prix pilots, how many potential World Champions can be seen? Senna, Prost, Mansell? Outsiders – Berger, Boutsen? Long-shot – Capelli? Whichever way you figure it, Nannini must be in with a good chance since most of the others in the cast are losers.

Sandro also has an extra incentive to do well. He is not the best-known Nannini in Italy. That honour belongs to his sister, Gianna. Terry Wogan has probably heard of her – she is one of Europe's top rock stars. She is also a motor-racing fan, especially when her brother is driving. Other young ladies who are Grand Prix *aficionados* had better look elsewhere than Sandro – he is happily married to Paola.

If Alain Prost reminds folk of the singer and actor Charles Asnavour, Nelson Piquet looks more like a male edition of Edith Piaf.

Piquet is the name of a card game for two, three or four players in which 32 cards are used. It is only the *assumed* name of the man who turned out to be one of motor-racing's greatest drivers and three times World Champion.

Nelson Souto Maior was born in Rio de Janeiro, Brazil, on 17 August 1952, to a family of comfortable means. Very athletic and keen on sport, the lad showed a great aptitude for tennis and rapidly became proficient at the game but someone introduced him to kart racing and gradually tennis receded into the background.

Motor-racing was now well and truly in his system but there was one major problem – his family. He knew his father would never approve of his new interest so he did what others have done before and will doubtless do again, he adopted a pseudonym to conceal his racing activites from his parent. The name he chose was 'Piket' or 'Piquet'. It was a name he was to

Niki Lauda – Benetton's Piquet 'learned a lot' from the Austrian World Champion.

116

Would you have known these drivers by their other given names? Teodorico, Marshall, McKay, Gianclaudio Giuseppe, Jacques-Bernard, Andreas-Nikolaus, Stanley, Simon-Wallis, Gabriele and Gabriele again?

In fact, they are best known as Teo Fabi (an easy one), John Watson, Eddie Cheever, Clay Regazzoni, Jacky Ickx, Niki Lauda, Alan Jones (Stanley after his father, famed Australian champion), James Hunt (now a British TV commentator), Riccardo Patrese and Mario Andretti.

make famous. He became Brasilia State 155cc kart champion; 2-litre sports-car champion; and finally Brazilian Super Vee Champon (six victories in ten races) before coming to Europe.

After an inauspicious start – he rolled a Formula 3 March at Zandvoort – he switched to

Ralt with great success. Third in the 1977 European Formula 3 Championship, he became British Champion the following year with the remarkable record of eight wins, three seconds and two fourth places in seventeen races and was runner-up for the British Vandervell Formula 3 Championship, winning five races out of nine.

Grand Prix drivers were once small boys with dreams who became young men with ambitions. Nelson Piquet was between dreams and ambitions when, in 1974, he spent a night guarding the Brabham garage at the non-Championship Brasilia Grand Prix. He was twenty-two at the time and dream and ambition fused into an enthusiasm for Brabhams which was to remain with him in the years he was decimating Formula 3.

Nelson Piquet in his Brabham days.

117

His first Formula 1 drive was not in a Brabham, however, but in one of Mo Nunn's Ensigns. Later he appeared in a BS Fabrications McLaren but his big moment came when Bernie Ecclestone offered him a third Brabham-Alfa for the 1978 Canadian Grand Prix. He was overjoyed and even more so when a contract followed as No. 2 to Niki Lauda. The Brazilian was delighted at the opportunity to work with the great Austrian, 'I learn a lot' he beamed.

'Admiral Nelson', as some called Piquet, did learn a lot – and he learned fast. He was already outspeeding Lauda quite often when the Austrian up-anchored and walked away from the Brabham team.

It was obvious from his first days with Brabham that Piquet was a Grand Prix driver of the highest class, his persistent and polished driving establishing him in the top rank. In 1980 he scored his first Grand Prix victory at Long Beach, California, and was runner-up in the World Championship to the Australian, Alan Jones. In 1981 Piquet won the title for the first time and in 1983 he won it again. Here he made a little motor-racing history because he thus became the first driver to win the World Championship in a turbocharged car, the Brabham-BMW.

In 1986 he joined the Williams team and in 1987 he won the World Championship for the

Reflection in the pits: Piquet waits to go out for practice.

third time and as the 1990s commenced was the only triple winner still active: Fangio, who actually won the title five times, Brabham, Lauda and Stewart having long retired. In 1988 he signed for Lotus, staying there two years until joining Benetton. Those two years will not feature as the happiest ones when he recalls his racing career to his grandchildren.

As a man Piquet is quiet and doesn't seek publicity, his interests lying in sailing, cruising and flying. He is a good test-driver and is popular with his mechanics. How many other drivers have a fan club which was founded by two of the mechanics?

As a driver there have been few to surpass him at his peak. McLaren Technical Director, Gordon Murray, for many years with Brabham, rated Piquet the best all-round driver of the 1980s. Prost, he felt, might have been just a shade quicker but Piquet still got Murray's vote. And Murray has worked with the best of them – Jack Brabham, Graham Hill, Jochen Rindt, Carlos Reutemann, Carlos Pace, John Watson, Alain Prost and Ayrton Senna, amongst others. Five of those, in addition to Piquet, have been World Champions.

This Piquet is, then, the man that many of the critics wrote off, after two disappointing seasons with Lotus, as a man who had lost the will to win. In so doing they conveniently overlooked the old saw about the jockey who couldn't go without the horse; Lotus had fallen from the grace of the great Chapman era, were switching from Honda to Judd engines and were going through all sorts of administration and personnel changes.

Although 1988 and 1989 were failures by Piquet's own high standards there are lots of other drivers on the circuits who would have liked to have done as well. In 1988, 'The Admiral' was sixth in the World Championship. In 1989 he was eighth – fourth in the Canadian, British and Japanese Grands Prix, fifth in the German and sixth in the Hungarian.

Trailing behind Piquet were such well-known names as Derek Warwick, Stefan Johansson, Michele Alboreto, Eddie Cheever, Andrea de Cesaris, Martin Brundle, Réne Arnoux, Jonathan Palmer and Philippe Alliot, a gaggle of others and the bright new rising star, Jean Alesi. If Piquet was finished, where did that leave them?

Piquet himself said: 'What people forget is that I have been around motor-racing all my life and I have nothing to do outside it. I want to try and win another championship.'

A man of whom the following was written must surely have enough stuff left in him to at least make a good bid for top honours in the Benetton colours:

'Has never driven better than he has this year – which means that he has no superior. A couple of equals maybe but no one in front of him. He is very quick, very consistent, good on all types of circuit – and as enthusiastic about his job as he was when he first started. That, in retrospect, is his greatest quality: he hasn't been submerged by the accruements of fame and has managed to concentrate on the things that matter to him.'

That was *Autocar*'s opinion of Piquet in July 1984. And that was the year John Watson, no mean driver himself, said:

'He just loves driving and gets on with it, without fuss. And he is a hell of a talented driver, a real natural. A really nice guy . . . and has a warm rapport with his team.'

A sentiment echoed by Michelin when they pulled out of Formula 1 . . . 'We will miss Piquet – he's good to work with.'

The years alter people, of course. Some seem to have seen more changes in Nelson than others. Five years later, there were people making remarks such as . . . 'Some love him (not many), some hate him.' On the other hand they were saying . . . 'Nelson is by no means finished. In a good car he will add to his GP victories.'

Benetton expect to provide that car with the assistance of Mr Ford.

119

Piquet's partner, Sandro Nannini, in Benetton's drive for the Championship.

If Nannini and Piquet don't do the job for Benetton what other drivers are likely to be available to the team during the early years of the last decade of the century? There is the obvious avenue of a high-powered transfer of a high-powered driver from another leading team.

However, leaving aside a transaction which would devolve largely around bags of gold and many of them, there is the possibility of Derek Higgins, a Benetton protégé, developing into a top-class driver especially since he has had the incentive of seeing his closest rival, Allan McNish, gain a three-year sponsorship from McLaren International and the almost certain promise of a Grand Prix chance should he improve as expected.

Then there is another Scot, Johnny Dumfries, whom Benetton have used as a test-driver without letting him loose in a race. Scion of a noble house, Johnny, who lives in Norfolk, must be tired of being described as a potential Grand Prix star and must hope that someone will stop talking about him long enough to give him an extended run in Formula 1. Born at Rothesay, Scotland, on 26 April 1958, time is slipping away for Johnny. No one wants a fairy – or a racing driver – when they're forty. Not unless their name is Juan Manuel Fangio.

No, the most likely to gain a regular Benetton drive may yet be one Johnny Herbert. Unless some other team snaps him up first. Which is very much on the cards. Tyrrell have already taken advantage of Benetton's hesitations to use Johnny in an emergency. When Benetton released him it was with the news that they hoped to keep him under contract, hoped to use him for testing in 1990 or place him with another

Allan McNish, who has stolen a march on Benetton protégé Derek Higgins in the race to get a Grand Prix seat.

Johnny Dumfries, who has worked for Benetton as a test driver but hankers after a Grand Prix seat.

Dumfries heads for victory in the Team BP Volkswagen Ralt, his fourth of the 1984 season.

team – and hoped to bring him back into their team in 1991.

In the sequel, Herbert signed with Lotus as a test and standby team driver for 1990 although Coloni and Eurobrun made offers. A fully-fit Herbert should be able to skate it in Formula 1 judging by his efforts half-crippled. He is already one of a very minute band of men who have scored points on their début in the World Championship – he was fourth in the Brazilian Grand Prix.

The last driver to have scored on his début was another young Briton, Martin Brundle, in 1984 though he was later disqualified. Prior to Martin, the list includes Alain Prost, Jim Clark, Jackie Stewart and Clay Regazzoni, certainly quality if not quantity.

Herbert, like so many race drivers today, started chasing about on four powered wheels at a very early age. Born in Romford, Essex, on 25 June 1964, son of an electrician, he was karting at the age of eight and British Junior Champion by the time he was fifteen. Some of the credit for this rubs off on 'Uncle Peter' who ran a kart track in Cornwall where young Johnny spent most of his time when the family were on holiday.

At eight, the young hopeful was the proud possessor of a 100cc machine of his very own. Soon he was racing competitively but officials

Clay Regazzoni – Benetton's Herbert joined him, Brundle, Prost, Clark and Stewart in scoring points on his Grand Prix début.

found out his age and in horse-racing parlance he was 'warned off'. It was but a temporary setback and by the time he was twelve he was racing nearly every weekend, his father acting as *chef d'equipe*, chief mechanic, personal adviser, head cook and bottle-washer and transport manager.

In 1978 Herbert was invited to join the Sisley works team and followed third place in the Championship race by winning the British Junior title the following season.

By 1981 he was a member of the British international squad and picked up another major championship along the way. A step-up to motor-racing proper was inevitable and it duly happened in 1983.

Herbert's career might have terminated early. A 1984 Formula Ford season which promised much looked like coming to an abrupt end when he crashed during a test session at the Cheshire track, Oulton Park. Part of the front suspension punched its way through Johnny's right leg, just above the knee. Miraculously, no bones were broken and he won his comeback race at Silverstone.

He joined the Quest Formula Ford team for 1985, narrowly missing out on the British Championship but gaining consolation by winning the Formula Ford Festival at Brands Hatch, a victory which ultimately led to him making his Formula 3 début at Donington in 1986. He finished fourth and his driving so impressed

Johnny Herbert: a lot of folk would like to see him overcome his bad luck and reach the Grand Prix heights.

An Irish bank official who has played a big role in bringing along young talent (including Benetton's Derek Higgins) was once an ambitious young driver himself. Eddie Jordan, born 30 March 1950, in Dublin, chucked up the safe security of a bank position to become a full-time racing driver.

After winning the Irish Kart Championship in 1973 he switched to racing cars proper and in 1978 won the Formula Atlantic Championships of both Eire and Northern Ireland. He made his Formula 3 début the same year.

He had a fantastic season – 11 wins, one second, three thirds; 12 pole positions, 12 fastest laps; and lap records at Kirkistown and Donington Park.

Later, Jordan formed his own team and operated with great success, Ayrton Senna and Jonathan Palmer being amongst his drivers.

team-owner Eddie Jordan, a shrewd Irishman, that he was signed up for Jordan's 1987 Formula 3 team.

With Jordan's guidance and driving an EJR Reynard, Johnny won six races in a row to take the British Formula Championship and also finished third in the prestigious Monaco Formula 3 race.

Lots of teams took an interest in him by now but Johnny remained loyal to Jordan. He began the 1988 season by dominating the opening round of the Formula 3000 series at Jerez, Spain, for a comfortable victory. Meanwhile, his Formula 3 Championship and win in the 1987 Formula 3 Superprix earned him a test drive in the Benetton Grand Prix car and it took

Reynard – the marque with which Johnny Herbert won the Formula 3 Championship.

only a handful of laps to demonstrate that here was a driver with the potential to be a Grand Prix star. Adapting immediately to the power and the road-holding of the Formula 1 car, Herbert stayed calm and self-assured, a natural talent if ever there was one.

However, a season which has begun brilliantly so nearly ended in tragedy. At Vallelunga, he was pushed into the wall and sustained severe concussion. Recovered, he had a much more serious accident. At Brands in August, his Reynard crashed head-on into the barrier at 170mph and he suffered severe leg and ankle injuries.

Despite this, Peter Collins and Benetton had enough faith in Herbert's natural ability to keep him as their No. 2 driver for the 1989 season and concentrated rehabilitation work had him behind the wheel again before Christmas, a tribute to the driver's spirit and determination. As leg injuries go, Herbert's could hardly have been worse. His ankles were shattered and his heels destroyed and the doctors discussed amputation. Benetton called in Tony Mathie, an Austrian 'keep fit' expert whose methods had aroused great controversy. Peter Collins, already under fire in the Italian press for signing a crippled British driver when there were plenty

A partnership which started well but didn't last the course. Sandro Nannini and Johnny Herbert with the Benetton Ford B189.

of young Italians available, ignored the critics. He was more concerned with getting Herbert fit.

Mathie used acupuncture, electrotherapy, ancient Chinese breathing exercises and much else besides and put Herbert through some gruelling – and painful – exercises. But the driver thought it was all worthwhile when they lifted him into a test car at Silverstone and he lapped in a time which would have put him on the ninth row of the grid in the previous season's British Grand Prix.

When the real thing came along in Brazil, this young driver who could hardly walk and was, in fact, an inch shorter than before his accident, gave a tremendous show of courage and skill. 'It was a tremendously brave effort,' said Nigel Mansell, 'he'll be great.'

And in that heat, Herbert's drink bottle had not worked all the race!

This is a man who could be the great racing star of the 1990s, or, like so many rising stars before him, he could disappear into obscurity. Those who know Johnny and his unquenchable spirit, those who have seen him display his undoubted driving skill, believe it will be the former. What no one knows is which car will provide him with a route to fame and fortune. Benetton? Or will Benetton rue him as the one who got away? Will Tyrrell or Lotus be the vehicle for his talents? Maybe Coloni or Eurobrun will have a car to match the man in a couple of seasons or so? Or maybe some other team, whose interest is not yet disclosed, will step into the picture?

Whether he comes back or not, Johnny Herbert's brief spell with Benetton certainly made headlines.

CHAPTER 9

AD 2000

Exciting times lie ahead for motor-sport in general and Benetton Ford in particular. No longer is motor-racing and its kindred activities a rather jolly pastime for 'the right crowd'. Instead it is a major industry and an important cog in the economic strength of the country, although it is seldom given credit for being so.

Figures released at the time of the 1990 Racing Car Show revealed that motor-sport in the UK has an annual turnover of more than £155 million of which at least £100 million is earned abroad in exports. Moreover the industry employs some 50,000 people, a useful slice of the working population. Nor do these figures give a full account since there are many facets of commerce and industry which overlap or link with motor-sport.

The UK is the world leader in the manufacture of racing cars. Some 90 per cent of all purpose-built racing cars, including most Formula 1 cars, are manufactured in the UK. Nearly 70 per cent of these cars are exported, including all the Indianapolis 500 racers – something which would have been unthinkable in the days when Hollywood dramas showed the special American-built Duesenbergs and Millers roaring across the screen, hurtling over the wall and generally turning the 'Old Brickyard' into a cinematic version of today's Australian soap operas.

For example, the Ilmor-Chevrolet-Penske, as American a sounding car as ever rode the silver screen, is now as British as they come. The Penske car, named after former Indy driver (and now an entrant), Roger Penske, is built in Poole, and the Ilmor modified Chevvy engine hails from Northampton.

And do all those hot-blooded Italian fans, screaming their heads off as the blood-red cars roar past, realise that Ferrari Formula 1 cars have a large UK input?

At the end of the day these race- and rally-tested components, designs and developments give birth to many features of production cars. Or to the like of Ford Special Vehicles such as the 1990 four-wheel drive 150mph Ford Sierra Sapphire Cosworth, available to the general public – or, at least, to those members of the general public with an odd £25,000 or so in their back pocket.

It does not stop there. Millions saw on television Nannini winning the third of Benetton's Grand Prix victories. Television coverage of motor-sport attracts more viewers in the UK than any other sport, except soccer. And, world-wide only the Olympics and World Cup soccer, beat it.

In 1989, the RAC Motor Sports Association licensed 236 car races, 327 kart races and 398 rallies and issued more than 31,000 competition licenses for all manner of events. Add to these figures those for all the other countries in the world where motor-sport takes place and one gains some idea of its worldwide popularity. There are precious few countries these days where no form of motor-sport takes place – and many where motor-racing in particular is an established part of the sporting scene – the US, France, Germany, Italy, Belgium, Holland, Australia, Japan. Nor can countries like Brazil, Argentina and New Zealand be omitted – countries which have produced racing drivers such as Fangio, Gonzales, Senna, Piquet, Brabham, McLaren, Amon, Hulme and the like.

The American racer, the Penske PC-6, designed by a Britisher, Geoffrey Ferris.

Geoffrey Ferris.

The successful American Penske with driver Rick Mears.

Roger Penske, famed Indianapolis driver and entrant.

One of the fastest cars in American auto racing through the 1980s was the Ford-powered Penske – designed by Geoffrey Ferris, who hails from Farnborough in Hampshire. The cars themselves were constructed at Poole in Dorset.

Why do the English so often hide their light under a bushel?

The end product, race and rally tested, the 1990 Ford Sierra Sapphire Cosworth.

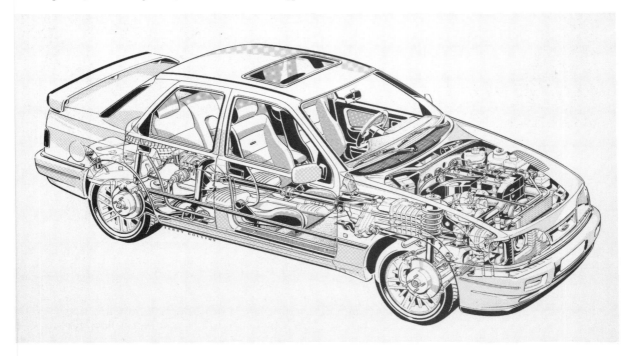

Sectionalised drawing of the Sierra Sapphire.

131

Millions saw Nannini win the third of Benetton's Grand Prix victories – via television.

Grand Prix racing in recent years has seen drivers from Colombia, Venezeula and Japan – only black drivers seem to have been in short supply so far. There have been one or two good black drivers in the US and a similar number who have shown promise in minor racing in the UK and doubtless their day will come.

Meanwhile, there will be quite enough strong opposition for Benetton Ford to contend with as the team battles through the last decade of the twentieth century. The team's plans are being made accordingly, because they realise that in the world's fastest sport no one ever got anywhere by standing still. Today's success is tomorrow's failure.

The public sees a couple of drivers and a couple of cars up front but, increasingly, success or failure depends upon the back-up behind the racers. Today's Grand Prix team manager is no longer a good egg in a flat cap who knows the best pub to stay at, rather he is a director of a large commercial concern, a man whose decisions can cost thousands, if not millions, of pounds if they don't work out.

No longer do teams set off from an old workshop or garage with just a couple of mechanics and, if they are lucky, a contract with an oil or tyre company. For example, Benetton employ 125 people at their Witney racing headquarters and when the team set off for a race the personnel number around 25. Those are the bare and basic figures but the operation is much more complicated than that. Progress in motorracing, as in ordinary motoring, has led to everything becoming more complicated and so the team has to be accompanied by a mass of technical equipment undreamt of just a decade or two ago. The transportation of all this equipment is further complicated when the team is not returning to base between races: for example, when the North and Central American races come close together or those in Japan and Australia.

For the European races it is comparatively easy, the team transporting almost everything in their own specially-constructed transporters, fitted with a great deal of equipment. Nor is it necessary to take so much in the way of spares because, in emergency, it is comparatively easy to obtain more.

The Grands Prix in far distant lands are much more of a problem despite the aircraft specially chartered for the task.

A breakdown of Benetton's task in sending the team to the Japanese and Australian Grands Prix shows that 88 typewritten sheets of paper had to be used to list the contents of 162 crates of spares and equipment valued in excess of £175,000.

The inventory included 10 spare engines, 80 wheels, a spare body shell, 60 sets of front and rear springs, scores of alternative gear ratios, 3 complete nose sections, 3 transmission rear-end assemblies, 8 clutches, 36 brake callipers, 17 master cylinders, 8 complete exhaust systems, 11 radiators, 13 sets of rear wings, a spare cockpit, 4 undertrays and a stock of nuts, bolts, screws, washers, clips and other odds and ends.

And *that* is only part of the story.

A couple of tool-kits and a jack might have been all right for Brooklands but the modern racing team has, in effect, to reproduce its home-base workshop at the circuit if the job is to be done properly.

Benetton send a crew of about twenty-five to every Grand Prix. Here is the team at the Hungarian race.

Leading the 1980 World Formula 2 Championship, the Toleman Group commissioned the ultimate in car transporters; an aerodynamically-efficient vehicle to act as workshop and transport for three racing cars. Design features were expected to bring a twenty-five per cent improvement in fuel efficiency. They included advanced aerodynamics for the whole outfit, careful choice of drive-line and the use of a new generation of Pirelli tyres which were not then commercially available. The unit to haul the transporter was a Ford Transcontinental HA4432, powered by the 'Big Cam' version of the Cummins NTE 350 (335) 14-litre Diesel. The engine was turbocharged and intercooled for maximum efficiency, producing 320bhp at 1,900rpm. Fuel consumption was anticipated to average ten miles per gallon. The trailer was built by Redment Engineering who had supplied the Toleman Group with more than 200 car transporter trailers during the previous two years. Streamlining was carried out by Fibre Flair, of Yaxley, Peterborough, and included an advanced roof side spoiler, roof spoiler, smooth underside to the trailer and enclosed sides to the unit between the wheels. Said Team Manager Roger Silman, 'Our new transporter will have a hard life. We have to keep to a tight schedule of practice sessions and races all over Europe and *the performance of the truck is almost as important as that of the cars.*

For the Benetton boys, heading for the lands of cherry blossom and Fosters lager, that means 7 working benches, 4 quick-lift jacks, 2 flat plates for use when setting up the cars and checking their corner weights, 3 portable generators, 7 battery chargers, 7 engine trolleys, 24 dry-cell batteries, 4 TV monitors and supporting electronic equipment.

In addition to normal oils, the cargo includes 42 gallons of engine oil, 20 gallons of gearbox oil and 120 bottles of brake fluid.

Then comes all the pit signalling equipment and working clothing: 3 sets of flameproof overalls, 5 helmets, 51 mechanics' overalls and 18 wet suits. The essential ingredient to enable all to keep going is, however trying the circumstances, the team's own coffee machine. And, to show that race teams can be as yuppie as anyone

else, a fax machine is carried, enabling communication with the outside world – even from darkest downtown Adelaide.

Oh, and we nearly forgot, three complete Benetton Ford racing cars and engines, without which the rest of the transportation exercise would be a waste of time.

However, that doesn't complete the task for the backroom boys and girls. The documentation has to satisfy the Customs and Excise and that means every single item – more than 1,000 – has to be described and valued, whether that value be thousands of pounds for an engine or a few pence for bin liners.

Not that there is very much in motor-racing which costs only a few pence. Just equipping a driver is quite an item. A good helmet at the time of writing (just the basic helmet unadorned) costs £345, a clear tinted fog-free visor £36, peak, side-plates and so on, £12 and a helmet bag £50 – giving a total approaching £450. And that's without a spare helmet.

A made-to-order professional race-suit will set someone back £420 plus 10 per cent, and made-to-measure in personalised design £499 plus 20 per cent. Gloves £55, boots £85, knee-length socks £10, Balaclavas £24, complete set of Nomex underwear £70. It's easy to see why in the Grand Prix game you need lots of money – or a wealthy sponsor.

If the mechanics are to do their job properly they need protection when the weather is bad (and we all know that whether or not it's the ozone layer, the nuclear warhead or the hot air emanating from the world's politicians it seems to be getting worse). That means wetsuit overalls for the lads and the prices for these come

Benetton Chief Mechanic, Nigel Stepney, is a dab hand with a fork-lift truck. On a notable occasion he managed to reverse one into a glass partition at the factory. At the annual Christmas dinner he was presented with a portion of the glass, mounted and inscribed by his fellow mechanics, 'We're only making panels for Nigel.'

out at about £80 each. Mechanics' overalls are around £38 each and that's without any logos or other decoration. Remember, Benetton take 51 of these on a long trip – just a little matter of a couple of thousand pounds.

Bearing in mind this is only fringe expenditure to the main expense of cars and engines it can be seen that a lot of capital is tied up in a Grand Prix team.

Obviously, a great deal of effort has to be put into just getting to a Grand Prix venue. Once there, it isn't just a matter of dumping the equipment and spares any old where. One area where little has changed over the years is the motor-racing pit. This remains a basically small and limited structure which means that efficient use must be made of it and even more of the paddock area behind. Usually transporters can be used as stores and workshops and refreshment rooms, and sometimes tents, marquees and caravans are pressed into service. A lot of work is also done in the open air.

The increase in technology also means that the hapless team manager has to find space for more personnel. Fortunately, Ford's electronic experts and their equipment can usually be tucked away in a quiet corner of the Ford marquee where they operate with quiet efficiency. With this sort of back-up in good working order, Gordon Message viewed Benetton's prospect in the 1990s . . .

'. . . with more confidence and enthusiasm than ever before. We are in the process of a major change of direction of which I am personally in full agreement. The biggest threats to our success are McLaren and Williams because of their resources, professionalism, forward planning and general perception of what is required.'

In fact, Benetton with John Barnard joining and Rory Byrne remaining, look to have the strongest 'think tank' in the business whilst on the circuit, should either Nannini or Piquet depart, Johnny Herbert may have another 'coming'. Despite the 1990 Lotus deal, Gordon Message confirmed that Johnny Herbert remained under contract to Benetton Formula Ltd and was on loan to Lotus for 1990. Other driver possibilities? It may give some light to know Gordon's opinions on the drivers who have driven for the Witney-based Toleman and Benetton teams during the 1980s. He doesn't hesitate.

The best? Without a doubt, that man of controversy, Ayrton Senna, of Brazil.

The easiest to work with? Unequivocally, Gordon plumps for the Briton, Derek Warwick.

For the moment and for some time to come, it looks as if Benetton have few driver and personnel problems. Nor do they have worries about power units. In addition to what the black-and-white print of the contracts may say, the Ford Motor Company has imposed upon itself a commitment to Formula 1 motor-racing which goes above and beyond purely commercial considerations. And while Benetton have the advantage of getting first crack at the latest developments in Ford engines, many other teams will benefit from the use of 'off the shelf' power units; 'off the shelf' in this case still being a quality product.

Ford's Michael Kranefuss summarizes his company's participation in the world of Grand Prix in this fashion:

'With 156 World Championship Grands Prix victories to their credit, Ford engines have been a vital ingredient in the success of Formula 1 for the past twenty-three years. From a victory first time out in the Dutch Grand Prix of 1967, the Ford DFV 3-litre V8 was powering its first World Championship driver and constructor in the following year, while the current Ford Formula 1 engine posted its first victory in the 1989 Japanese Grand Prix.

'In conjunction with Cosworth Engineering, Ford is providing its latest 3.5-litre Formula V8 exclusively to Benetton Formula for Alessandro Nannini and Nelson Piquet while the Ford DFR V8 engine is being made available to a

Designer Rory Byrne at work. With John Barnard it gives Benetton the strongest 'think tank' on the circuits.

The Benetton Ford partnership extends outside motor racing. The speedy Ford Fiesta R S Turbo has upholstery and seats all trimmed in Benetton 'Ascot' fabric.

number of other Formula 1 teams contesting the World Championship.

'Electronics now play a major role in the design of a modern Formula 1 car and in this highly-specialized field of activity, Ford Electrical and Electronics Division has established a world lead over its competitors. Ford research into advanced materials, suspension and power units, is using Formula 1 as a means of accelerating investigations, development and research for future generations of volume production Ford cars.'

Which is proof, if proof be needed, that motor-

racing is still, in the words of the MG Company, many years ago, 'Improving the breed.'

Ford also regard their Formula 1 programme as helpful in training personnel. Says Kranefuss, 'Ford engineers are now able to take full advantage of the disciplines and deadlines of participation in Formula 1 as a vital part of their training and education.'

But perhaps most important to the future of motor-racing in general and Benetton in particular is Ford's great affinity with motor-sport. As Michael Kranefuss says:

'Ford remains committed to direct participation

137

in World Championship Formula 1 *for rather more than the publicity and promotion of its products* and its world-wide expertise in engineering.'

Nor will Formula 1 in the 1990s be dependent entirely upon Ford power. Porsche are back in the fray after a couple of seasons out of Grand Prix racing, Honda, Ferrari and Renault are already powers in the land and then there are Judd, Yamaha and Lamborghini, whose full potential has yet to be realised.

It won't be easy, given such competition, but from Ford radiates a quiet confidence and a feeling that Nannini's victory in the 1989 Japanese Grand Prix may have been the start of another record 150 plus run. It is a confidence echoed in the Benetton team which faces at least the next few years without sponsorship worries, unlike some of the other Formula 1 teams.

As long as World Championship motor-racing continues to attract world-wide television coverage there will be companies prepared to sponsor teams. It is, however a limited fishing ground from which to trawl, so vast are the sums required to run a team, successful or otherwise.

Fortunately, the beer and tobacco barons, faced with restrictions on advertising in many countries, continue their support for the travelling billboards of the Grand Prix circus. To their number has been added an increasing number of Japanese companies, the Japanese acquiring motor-racing teams with the same avidity as they swallow up golf courses. This has led to the inclusion of a handful of Japanese drivers in Grand Prix teams although at the time of writing, only one, Satoru Nakajima, has managed to score points, driving for the Lotus team.

The 1990s look, then, like being colourful and exciting times in Grand Prix racing and because the Benetton team is amongst the most colourful and most exciting of all the *equipes* it may well be the team of the decade. Certainly, there is no lack of confidence at Witney or in Benetton HQ in the cars, the designers, the

engines and – whatever some critics may say – the drivers.

However, in the world of sport today the physical capacity of individuals or teams is not enough to reach and maintain the highest level of success. Money is required and the only way to obtain the kind of money necessary is by maximum exposure through the media, especially television, and the exploitation of all sources of revenue.

Sport in general was fairly slow in realising this hard fact of life. Soccer, for example, relied mainly on the gate money with a little help from the sales of advertisements in the match programme and the local grocer donating the match ball on Saturdays. As for the players, they took their wages and as they grew older looked around for a corner shop or a little pub against the harsh day when their services were no longer required.

County cricket was even less commercially minded. No ads on the scorecard although one or two of the top players, Denis Compton and Keith Miller, for instance, might make a few quid appearing in hair-cream advertisements.

So it was with nearly every sport. Motor-racing, although by its very nature more expensive than most sports, was among the more lethargic in moving with the times. Tra-

---

Additional sponsorship backing for Benetton in 1990 came from a most remarkable Japanese company, Nippon Autopolis Company.

In addition to their team sponsorship it was expected that the company would bid to stage the Japanese Grand Prix at their new circuit on the slopes of the extinct volcano, Mount Aso Kusu. The 22-cornered circuit is 2.9 miles (4.7km) in length. It could not be considered as a Grand Prix venue before 1992; Suzuka having a contract for 1990 and 1991.

Autopolis is not just a racing circuit but perhaps an indication of the future. It forms just part of a resort and leisure complex which includes tennis courts and ski slopes with artificial snow.

Nor is that all. There are shops – doubtless stocking Benetton goods – and, believe it or not, an art gallery with many masterpieces including some by artists Picasso and Renoir.

ditionally, most motor-racing teams were an adjunct of a car manufacturer – Bugatti, Mercedes, Maserati, Alfa Romeo and the like; a few were wealthy private entrants; and, on the odd occasion, someone outside the sport might 'sponsor' a team, although the term was not in use in those days. One example was wealthy racehorse owner, the Hon. Dorothy Paget, who

was once persuaded by Sir Henry 'Tim' Birkin to put up the cash for a team of Bentleys.

The drivers, too, were predominantly amateur but both drivers and teams relied for some support on the tyre and oil companies, sparkplug manufacturers and others, all 'insiders' in the world of motoring.

It was quite some time after the Second

Jackie Stewart (seen here with Ken Tyrrell and members of his team) was one of the first drivers to realise that the world was his oyster – if his affairs were handled well.

139

World War that sport in general realised the scope there was in cash and promotional support from the great big world outside and even longer before it realised that there was also money to be made in marketing goods associated with the individual sportsman, the team or the cars, planes, motorboats, cycles and so on.

In the 1960s and 1970s motor-racing began to wake-up and sponsors of all kinds began to come into the sport. Jackie Stewart was one of the first of the Grand Prix racers to realise that the world was his oyster. The present writer recalls talking with Jackie at Silverstone when he turned around and said, 'Have you met Mr So-and-so from the Mark McCormack Organisation? They represent me now.'

Jackie had signed up with the American entrepreneur who had made his name by showing the big stars of American golf how to cash in on their tournament successes. The Scot's shrewd move led to what amounted to a Jackie Stewart industry which continued to provide Jackie with a hard-working, jet-setting but lucrative livelihood long after he had retired from the circuits. Though Jackie was not the first motor-racing ace to have an agent, he and McCormack blazed the way in showing just what could be done. Up until that time, most agents contented themselves with book contracts, personal appearances and the like.

What Jackie did for drivers, a former London motorbike dealer did for the sport as a whole. One-time Brabham owner, Bernie Ecclestone, became the most powerful man in the sport. He organized the car constructors, tied-up the TV contracts and, in a nutshell, brought about a situation where, if anyone wanted to participate in a competitive Grand Prix, they had to go through Bernie. He would deliver the complete package and, in so doing, he took Formula 1 racing into the big time.

Bernie had to fight hard to do so. He said to this author once:

'The main trouble is that everyone in the game is looking after themselves instead of looking at matters overall. If the overall picture is right then we shall all be right individually. Alas, some of them can't see that. They just look for the short-term results. Of course, some of them are owned by companies and you can understand the pressures on them.'

Bernie eventually won the day and the money came flooding into Grand Prix racing. FISA, the controlling body of motor-racing sport, the body created by Bernie known as the Formula One Constructors' Association (FOCA) grew closer together; and the forecast of Dean Delamont, then head of the RAC's motor-sport activities was fulfilled. Dean had said that Bernie's efforts would give the race organizer the opportunity of getting a proper package, would aid sponsorship negotiatons, help television coverage and help generally towards the popularity of the sport. All of which, more or less, has come true.

Just the same, the smart team and the smart driver will realise that it can't all be left to someone else. The Lord helps those who help themselves, as the old saying goes. So today, the outfit aiming for the top will have commercial and marketing managers, press and PR consultants, publicity and promotion executives – in a word or two, ideas men and women.

Benetton head into the 1990s with all of these attributes wrapped in a one-man package, a live-wire personality, reared in the hard world of 'rag trade' sales but working for an organization where colour and glamour and beauty all have their place.

Flavio Briatore, born 12 April 1950, in Verzolo, Italy, is the man charged by the Benetton organization with making sure that their investment in motor-racing is a commercial as well as a sporting success and that Benetton deeds on the racetrack wil be reflected in sales in Benetton shops. He is sure that the right groundwork has been done to ensure that the team puts up a good show in the 1990s. He says:

'We have completely changed the team. Now,

Flavio Briatore, director of Benetton Formula Limited, the man whose job it is to see that racing pays off.

Luciano Benetton, whose dream it was, and his son Alessandro, President of Benetton Formula Limited

technically we are very strong and we are going to be stronger because we have secured the services of John Barnard from Ferrari. Our new Technical Centre under John's direction will be located at Godalming (Surrey).'

'I asked Briatore: 'Is Rory Byrne staying with you now that John Barnard has joined you?' He replied:

'I hope so. Rory is a brilliant designer. I think he is happy with us and I think he is going to stay. He certainly is as far as we are concerned.

'However, today you have to realise that the top designers like Rory are very much in demand. Just as much as the best race-drivers. They can move around in the same way. There is always someone who is prepared to offer more money or offer a more attractive assignment.

'But we think the sweeping changes we have made will help to keep our people together. We deliberately set out to create a younger team than we had before and, most importantly, a more professional one. We are satisfied that we have achieved both.'

I asked Briatore what else remained to be done. He answered: 'To win the World Championship.'

That, of course, is far easier said than done. When FISA announced the drivers and teams who would start off Grand Prix racing in the 1990s, Benetton-Ford were confronted by 18 other teams and 33 drivers.

Some of these might not last a season, others have been around for years and, barring earthquakes, hurricanes and pestilence, will almost certainly be around in AD 2000. Some are obvious World Championship contenders, others no-hopers, although assertions at both ends of the scale can, in the words of Confucius, leave 'muchee egg on face'.

The drivers are, if anything, more of a mixture than the cars. There is a big turnover in drivers in Grand Prix racing every ten years, or

so it seems. Thus, in the final decade of the century there are drivers who have been at the top for a long while now, some who have never made it, others usefully embarked upon careers where, hopefully, the best is yet to come, and others who are young, willing and have stars in their eyes.

Benetton's up-and-coming Nannini and experienced top-liner Piquet, backed by Benetton cars and Ford engines, is a formidable mixture; many other teams do not have anything like such a well-balanced look. Yet who wants balance if you have great cars and two great drivers?

Thus McLaren started the 1990s as they ended the 1980s – at the top of the tree although even they have been forced to realise that some of the opposition is distinctly cheeky. McLaren lost Alain Prost (which could be a relief after the 'Civil War' with Senna) and they also lost Steve Nichols from their design team, the quiet-spoken man from Utah apparently not too happy that he had not been appointed Chief Designer. Nevertheless, with Senna and Gerhard Berger handling the powerful V10 Hondas, Ron Dennis could still look forward to continued success even if not by the overwhelming margins which had threatened to reduce Grand Prix racing to a bore as the 1980s faded into limbo. Nor would cash be a problem for a team backed by Marlborough and Honda (the Japanese firm alone is rumoured to spend one hundred million dollars per year on Formula 1 racing).

The team which could match the McLarens in the contents of its bank vault is Ferrari. The Italian *equipe*, owned by multi-millionaire Giannini Agnelli and his Fiat organization, goes into the 1990s with the boss-man saying that he wants championships and lack of money is not to be an excuse. If it is genuinely needed it will be forthcoming. No one doubts it. The sport-loving Italian tycoon has poured millions into his soccer teams – and they are just a hobby. Where cars are concerned, Fiat have more than a passing interest in securing victory over the Japanese.

Alain Prost, whose struggle with Ayrton Senna highlighted the end of the eighties, as a very youthful Formula 3 Renault driver.

143

Ferrari, too, have lost a designer but they have also gained one, the aforementioned Mr Nichols from McLaren. They also have a new driver, the aforementioned Mr Prost from McLaren. Whatever Ferrari lack in the 1990s it should not be knowledge of their main opposition . . .

Prost is undoubtedly still a fine driver and might well be the perfect foil to the charging Brit from Brum, Nigel Mansell, golfing protégé of Greg 'White Shark' Norman and arguably the fastest Grand Prix driver in the world today, a man his fellow countrymen hope can bring back the glory days when Stewart, Clark, Hill, Hawthorn, Moss and company were on top of the pile.

These two teams, plus Williams, are the trio which Benetton-Ford must overcome if the hopes of the Anglo–Italian set-up are to be realised in this decade. Williams know well the sweet smell of success and with the proven Renault V10 engine bolted into the Patrick Head chassis their chances remain good. Some doubt the ability of Thierry Boutsen and Riccardo Patrese in relation to the Senna–Berger and Mansell–Prost combinations but it is unlikely that either McLaren or Ferrari will brush off the Williams men too lightly. If the Williams machinery is reliable enough and fast enough Boutsen and Patrese are good enough.

If Benetton Ford have to look over their shoulder while chasing the top three, it may be that they will see Lotus, Tyrrell or Arrows chasing them. These are three more very experienced teams and Lotus and Tyrrell have tasted life at the top and badly want to do so again.

Camel Team Lotus took the first steps in 1990 with a smaller, sleeker but slightly longer car, the Lotus 102, masterminded by Frank Dernie. The most significant change was in the power unit, the Judd V8 engine having been dropped in favour of the more powerful Lamborghini V12 which made its Grand Prix début in 1989.

Colin Chapman, Lotus team founder, was noted for his efforts to achieve maximum per-

formance by lightening the car. It was a standing joke that if Colin could find an inch of chassis that wasn't doing anything in particular he would drill a hole through it. With the Lamborghini engine heavier than the Judd and requiring more fuel, Dernie had to go back to the old days and lighten everything he could. 'We even saved half a kilo by making Derek Warwick a special lightweight helmet ourselves, using the manufacturer's moulds,' laughed Frank. The old guv'nor would have been proud of him.

> Lions may not lie down with lambs in modern Grand Prix racing but they have been known to associate with tigers. Camel Team Lotus began the 1990s with Lamborghini engines. The parent Lotus Group is owned by General Motors, the Italian Lamborghini firm by one of GM's big rivals, Chrysler . . .

In its first Formula 1 season the Italian-made engine (built under the direction of Mauro Forghieri, the man who was Ferrari's technical chief for more than twenty years) qualified and started in every one of the sixteen races. Also, in the second half of the 1989 season, driver Philippe Alliot was consistently in the front half of the starting grid – gaining Lamborghini's first point in the Spanish Grand Prix. It was encouraging for Lotus. The Norfolk team had two new drivers, three if the reserve is counted, in Derek Warwick, Martin Donnelly and Johnny Herbert, who had made a promising start to his Grand Prix career with Benetton.

Warwick, who started in Formula 1 with Toleman, joined Lotus from Arrows, a difficult situation for an essentially loyal driver who had had three years with the Arrows team. He had always cherished a feeling that he might drive for Lotus and indeed had twice before nearly joined the team. The first time was at the end of his first season with Renault when he had offers from both Lotus and Williams. He said:

Derek Warwick tries out the 1990 Camel Lotus 102 Lamborghini. Martin Donnelly and Frank Dernie look on.

'That was when I made the biggest mistake of my career. Although I have no regrets I decided to stay with Renault and they went into decline. Then I had the saga at the end of 1985 when Lotus wanted me but Ayrton Senna (then Lotus No. 1) was against it and I did some sports-car racing before signing with Brabham. For the last three years I was with USF & G

> One-time powerboat racer, Clive Chapman, is a backroom boy at Camel Team Lotus. He is the son of Colin Chapman, founder of the Lotus team. The son has followed his father's interest and has a degree in Mechanical Engineering from London's University College.

Arrows and the team developed from a top ten team to a top five team in that time. I like to think I had something to do with that.'

Warwick was encouraged to line up with Lotus by the shake-up in the team management. 'Now I feel the team is young and dynamic,' he said, 'ready to get back to being what it was when Colin Chapman was alive.' He also said:

'Having the Lamborghini engine is great – it has so much potential. If you don't have a manufacturer behind you, you are in Division Two on the racetrack. With the V8 engine many of the teams have now, instead of challenging for the top placings you have to inherit them. With the

Lamborghini engine it should be different. The reliability they should have will give Lotus a real chance to compete with the Division One teams such as McLaren, Williams and Ferrari.

Warwick's partner, Martin Donnelly, promoted from reserve and test-driver the previous season, is one of the newcomers on whom a lot of attention may be focused in the 1990s. Another graduate of the Eddie Jordan 'school of racing', he was Irish Formula Ford 2000 Champion in 1983, second in the British Championship in 1985 with seven victories, voted 'most promising British driver' in 1987 and won the Macau Formula 3 Grand Prix, FIA F3 World Championship.

Benetton tested Donnelly in 1988 and he made his first Grand Prix appearance the following year when he replaced the injured Warwick in the Arrows team, finishing twelfth in the French Grand Prix after starting the race from the pitlane in the spare car.

Arrows, the team Warwick left, might well emerge as the danger team of the decade, having signed a four-year agreement with the legendary German Porsche team. Whilst the benefits of this partnership might not be immediately apparent it is understood that a new Porsche V12 engine under development would be available to the Arrows in 1991. Meanwhile Arrows could yet be a force with their expanded premises, new sponsors (Footwork), an established front-rank driver (Michele Alboreto) and one rated more promising by Frank Williams and others. He is Alex Caffi, also an Italian, born on 18 March 1964. Caffi did well with lowly Scuderia Italia and has known the heady delights of a top ten finish.

Tyrrell Racing have suffered for some years over a lack of consistent high-powered sponsorship and, not unnaturally, this has affected their results. But the know-how is there and the Surrey team is always likely to spring a surprise – or maybe two. They started the 'final decade' campaign with the much-vaunted Jean Alesi plus Japan's first full-time Grand Prix driver,

Satoru Nakajima, who switched to Tyrrell after a steady spell with Lotus during which he managed to finish amongst the points on occasion. But, at 37, he is not likely to make any startling improvement.

Most of the other teams and drivers in the field as Grand Prix racing moved into the final decade of the century were very much of the minnow category but their hopes ran high – after all even Division One teams have to start somewhere. Of those most likely to make the grade some day the Leyton House team and those capable March drivers, Mauricio Gugelmin and Ivan Capelli, look the best bet.

Gugelmin, born in Brazil on 20 April 1963, made a sound début in 1988 (highest place fourth) and was rated by the experts as highly promising. Capelli, of similar age but more experience, was born in Italy on 24 May 1963, and has been as high as runner-up in the placings. Many rate him a very fine driver indeed and not a few experts have tipped him as a potential World Champion. They are certainly a pair to be watched.

Some former Benetton and Toleman pilots are scattered amongst the rest of the hopefuls, no hopers and 'just for the ride' conductors but, truth to tell, most of them are not expected to rate highly in world rankings as the seasons speed by to AD 2000.

Emmanuele Pirro, who had a half-season with Benetton without unduly troubling the front-runners, got another stab at Formula 1 by taking the seat at Scuderio Italia left vacant by Alex Caffi. He joined the incumbent veteran of the Grand Prix wars, the 31-year-old Italian, Andrea de Cesaris – one of the most travelled competitors in the business, having been with McLaren, Alfa, Ligier, Minardi, Brabham and Rial prior to joining Scuderia Italia. A contemporary said of him: 'Fast on his day and well connected.' Then added with a sigh, 'Otherwise he usually connects with the scenery.'

Stefan Johansson pursues his strange odyssey via good, bad and mediocre teams, starting the 1990s with Moneytron Onyx, his partner in

Martin Donnelly who tried out with Benetton and found a spot with Lotus.

whatever might lie ahead, the Finnish driver, J. J. Lehto. Johansson is almost as much a mystery as Philippe Alliot who pursues a similar lonely furrow. Alliot, born on 27 July 1954, began the decade partnered in the Ligier team by a promising Italian, Nicola Larini. Alliot is hardly likely to improve, Larini, at 26, could conceivably make the grade.

A fast driver is 28-year-old Bertran Gachon. Just how fast the world is not likely to find out while he cuts his Grand Prix eye teeth at first Onyx and then Subaru Coloni.

The nearly man, Roberto Moreno, born in Brazil on 11 February 1959, who has so often missed out on good drives – unlike his more illustrious compatriots such as Piquet and Senna – finally got into Formula 1 with Coloni then moved to the Swiss–Italian team of Eurobrun with Claudio Langes in the other seat.

France's hope for the future is probably Yannick Dalmas, a star in junior formulae but whose senior career was interrupted when he contracted legionnaires' disease. He has scored in Grands Prix (which is more than some of his rivals) but moved from one French team to another, Larrousse to AGS, his partner at the latter being Gabriele Tarquini.

Espo Larrousse, after a lot of troubles, went into the 1990s with Eric Bernard and a rather wild Japanese gentleman, Aguri Suzuki, who returned to the team after a spell with Zakspeed.

Minardi keep going with the indefatigable Pierluigi Martini, aided and abetted by Paolo Barilla; Osella went along with French-born Olivier Grouillard, a man with a good record as a test-driver.

Brabham, with the glory days gone, at least for a time, persevered with a talented young Italian, Stefano Modena, and a Swiss driver, Gregor Foitek. And, talking of Brabham, past memories were revived with the entry into the lists of Sir Jack Brabham's son, Gary, the middle one of three racing sons, Geoffrey, Gary and David. Gary was entered by Life Racing.

In addition to these drivers there are a number of others about with Grand Prix experience and a great many more who would give anything for a chance at the big time.

Joachim Winkelhock, of Germany; Eddie Cheever, having a sabbatical in American oval racing and sports cars; British test drivers Johnny Herbert and Johnny Dumfries; Martin Brundle, former World Sports-Car Champion; Pierre-Henri Raphanel, of France; the veteran René Arnoux; Piercarlo Ghinzani, another in the veteran stage; the competent German, Christian Danner, and his countryman Volker Weidler, another taking a sabbatical in sports cars; Bernd Schneider; and Britain's experienced Dr Jonathan Palmer; these are the known Grand Prix drivers who may yet play a role in the 1990s although in some cases age or disillusionment may keep them out of the game.

Alas, it is all very much a lottery and the cast of minor characters among the minor teams is subject to constant change with hard cash playing a major role.

There are two ways to the heart of a Grand Prix team. One is to be a brilliant driver, aglow with so much talent that no team owner could resist you. The other is to be a driver of any description arriving with large bags of gold, shares in oil wells or the equivalent. Whether the money is your own or that of some kind sponsor doesn't really matter as long as it is ready and available. Should you turn out to be a good driver as well as having lucrative sponsorship then that is a lucky bonus for the team.

An example: Gregor Foitek, the Swiss Formula 3000 driver, broke into Formula 1 with the Eurobrun team. When he signed for Brabham he was reported to have brought with him $1¼ million in sponsorship which was more than the other main contender, Luis Perez Sala, a Spanish driver formerly with Minardi, could produce. This, inevitably, is bound to be the pattern when motor-racing is so expensive. The days are long gone when a couple of enthusiasts could buy a second-hand BRM or Cooper, tweak it a bit and, in a rags to riches fairy tale, drive it to victory in at least a non-championship Grand Prix.

148

Fortunately, as the next ten years stretch out ahead this is not the sort of problem greatly exercising the Benetton and Ford partnership. If only . . . if only they can get the mixture of car, engine and driver right then the world title that Gordon Message and Flavio Briatore dream of might be within reach. Time will tell . . .

The first Grand Prix of the 1990s began in an atmosphere of the biggest hype imaginable. Not in the US, however, host country of the race, where excitement was at something below room temperature – the organizers were offering free admission to pre-qualifying sessions and a cut-price $200 package covering the three days of practice qualifying and racing – but in the rest of the world, not least in the UK, it was a different story.

The British national and Sunday press has never given such space to motor-sport. It was almost as if the mandarins of Wapping, Battersea, parts of Fleet Street and various other points north, west, south and east had suddenly discovered Grand Prix racing.

Colour photos of every car, pen portraits of every driver, colour supplements, post-mortems on Senna versus Prost last season and previews of Senna versus Prost this season, analysis of why Mansell would be champion driver in 1990, analysis of why Mansell would *not* be champion driver this season, how much money Mansell earned last year (£6 million, the scribe thought) compared with how much money Stirling Moss earned in his best year (it was 1961 and Moss said he made £31,000. Then, the equivalent to the pay of a top surgeon).

Benetton, from a racing point of view if not the publicity angle, must have been relieved that most of the pundits either had not heard of them or alternatively did not fancy their chances. At least it kept off a little of the pressure. There were so many press conferences being held that a diligent scribe could have managed breakfast, lunch and dinner at somebody's expense almost every day in the run-up to the opening struggle.

Television added to the build-up with Eurosport announcing a new deal for satellite viewers – the most comprehensive coverage of Formula 1 motor-racing ever seen on television.

After several weeks of discussion with Bernie Ecclestone and FOCA, Eurosport announced that they would 'take the helmets off the drivers' and go behind the scenes for the latest news and views from the track. (They did not announce any reaction from Jean-Marie Balestre, President of the FIA and President of FISA to their statement that FOCA is 'the sport's governing body.')

Christian Vogt, FOCA spokesman, commented:

'Eurosport came to us with the idea of showing all the facets of Grand Prix motor racing. They'll be going behind the scenes and meeting the teams – on and off duty – as well as capturing the drama of Friday's qualification, Saturday's official practice and, of course, the whole of every race *live*. Eurosport has taken an innovative step which is crucial to the further development of Formula 1 motor-racing.'

The countdown begins on Friday evenings, focusing on the battle for qualification, with comment from the drivers, their wives, their girl-friends (both at the same time?) pit-crews and everyone connected with the world of Formula 1. Each week, on-board cameras give viewers a breathtaking ride around the Grand Prix circuit.

On Saturdays, the cameras focus on the mounting tension as the drivers compete for

> One-time Toleman Team Manager, Roger Silman, was mugged when the team was in Rio for the Brazilian Grand Prix. Out for the evening with a young lady friend, he was confronted by a local 'gentleman' who made a grab for the lady's handbag. When Roger intervened he was stabbed and wound up in hospital – an experience not to be repeated according to Roger, the hospital being almost as frightening as the mugger.

positions on the grid; on Sundays they will present the whole race; and every Tuesday evening Eurosport will screen highlights of every race, post-race stories and interviews.

Production controller Richard Russell said:

'For far too long television coverage of Grand Prix motor-racing has started just ten minutes before a race and finished at the chequered flag. Now we plan to provide the sort of coverage that the drivers themselves are keen to see – capturing the humour of the sport as well as all the drama and tension.'

Away from all the ballyhoo and sensationalism, Gordon Message was looking forward to the season with quiet confidence. He wasn't too sure about the first race for reasons that will emerge later but having ended the 1989 season with victory in Japan and second place in Australia he felt that Benetton Ford had every ground for optimism.

For the opening round (and the next Grand Prix in Brazil a fortnight later) the team would have three B189s, last year's cars with a number of modifications aimed at improving performance, largely in the fields of aerodynamics and suspension and – not least – the new Ford V8 engine which had been undergoing intensive development during the off-season.

Cosworth's Dick Scammell commented:

'The Ford F1 engine which Benetton will use during the first part of the season will be a new third generation model. It is now developing an additional 25hp compared to the power unit which was used to win the 1989 Japanese Grand Prix. Design changes to the oil system, camshafts, valve gear and the camshaft drive gears will provide the drivers with an additional 250rpm. Further changes are under development and a Series 4 engine is planned for the second half of the season.'

After the Brazil race, it was planned that testing would begin with the new car, the B190, the

work of Chief Designer Rory Byrne, with some input from Technical Director John Barnard. Incidentally, the team now had an additional race engineer on the payroll, Georgio Ascanelli, another from the Ferrari *equipe*.

For 1990 the first race of the season was in that hotbed of Hollywood cowboy and Indian 'fillums', Arizona, to whit, the capital city of Phoenix. The previous year the Phoenix race has been the fifth in the series and experience then led Gordon to be doubtful about the outcome this time. He made no bones about it. 'The race is a lottery,' he said.

The crux of the situation was the very nature of the circuit . . .

A 1990 portrait of John Barnard.

A 1990 portrait of Rory Byrne.

In length 2.36 miles (3.8km), the Phoenix circuit winds its way through the commercial district of the city (a bit different from the City of London where, unless things have changed recently, there are no mountains roundabout) but the main hazards are eleven, almost right-angle bends and the concrete retaining walls. 'Disaster lurks around every corner,' said a Nigel Mansell in unusually poetic mood.

In 1989, although Herbert brought one Benetton from the back row of the grid to fifth place, bouncing off the concrete walls did no good at all, either for Nannini or his car.

That there was good reason for Gordon Message's and Mansell's forebodings came as the cars got on the track for pre-qualifying and practice.

They spun here, they spun there – and the unlucky ones collected a wall in the course of their gyrations although fortunately no one was badly hurt. Lotus newcomer Martin Donnelly lost his front end, Ligier's Alliot, his rear. His team-mate Larini, the Japanese Satoru Nakajima and Morbidelli (Scuderia Italia) were others to suffer damage. Michele Alboreto, in his Arrows, and Benetton's 'new' man, Nelson Piquet, also spun but managed to avoid the walls.

Others had a happier time, Roberto Moreno (Eurobrun), Eric Bernard and Aguri Suzuki, the two Larousse-Lola drivers, and Olivier Grouillard (Osella) all put up good times in pre-qualifying although, alas, Gary Brabham, beset by electrical problems, only managed four un-satisfactory laps. Most people were a little sad about that. Although the ever popular Sir Jack Brabham had three motor-racing sons it was the first time that the Brabham name had figured in Grand Prix driver entry list since Jack himself had retired from the scene twenty years previously. Gary Brabham was not the only driver to be disappointed. Former Benetton driver, Emanuele Pirro, was a non-starter through hepatitis, his place being taken by Giovanni Morbidelli.

With due respect to the drivers and cars concerned these were matters of minor importance. Most attention was focused on Senna – had the events of the winter and last season affected his consummate skills? On Prost – now he was driving for a rival team could he again beat Senna and bid for another world title? On Mansell – was 1990 to be his year as had so often been predicted? Or would it be the year when Thierry Boutsen finally came into his own? And was Benetton's Piquet really washed-up as some wiseacres affirmed?

There was also a sort of supporting feature. The battle of the tyre manufacturers had resumed in earnest with Goodyear and Pirelli the protagonists. Goodyear arrived in Phoenix with 2,160 tyres which included two types of potential race tyres, both a little softer than the type

*Two men expected to figure prominently in the nineties. Thierry Boutsen (then with Benetton)
and Alain Prost (then with McLaren) battle it out during the 1988 San Marino Grand Prix.*

used in the corresponding race the previous year. Their rain tyres were the same as before but the qualifying tyres were a new construction. Pirelli had some 900 tyres on hand with three different types of race tyre, two of them new, and the same qualifiers as in 1989. Their challenge to Goodyear supremacy had been strengthened by the Tyrrell team switching to the Italian tyres for the next two seasons at least.

Adding piquancy to the battle was the fact that street circuits like Phoenix are usually more demanding on tyres by their very nature and the high summer temperatures of Arizona are an additional factor. Pirelli were certainly happy during Friday's pre-qualifying when some good performances were put up with Pirelli-shod cars.

One of them, the Minardi of Pierluigi Martini, kept up the good work to such good effect that there was a major surprise, something unheard of in World Championship racing, a Minardi on the front row of the grid alongside the customary sight of a McLaren. And even the McLaren was not the anticipated one of Senna but his new team-mate Gerhard Berger.

Blazing sunshine was conspicuous by its absence as race time drew near and the Phoenix circuit with its high drab concrete walls looked more like a movie set for Alcatraz than a Grand Prix race circuit. Nor had it attracted the local populace in great numbers. The crowd was bigger than in 1989 but still not as large as at most Grand Prix circuits around the world. In truth the American motor-sport *aficionado* has not yet been fully convinced about the merits of Grand Prix racing – Indianapolis and stock cars both have greater appeal. Nor are there any all-American heroes like Mario Andretti and Dan Gurney to inspire patriotic fervour– even Eddie Cheever has moved along. And the prospect of roast rattlesnake on the restaurant menus doesn't really offset the claustrophobic atmosphere generated by this strangest of motor-race venues.

Still with the reservation that the race would

be a lottery, there was quiet confidence in the Benetton team as the green-overalled mechanics wheeled out No.19 for Nannini and No. 20 for Piquet. The Williams team seemed happy and one or two of the lesser lights were positively bubbling. McLaren showed a determination to put the events of the past fifteen months behind them. 'We will deliver our response in the right place – out on the track,' said team chief Ron Dennis.

However, he could not resist a comment on the reports that Ferrari's testing programme indicated 'The Prancing Horse' would be the favourite in 1990. 'Ferrari have a tradition of winning the *winter* world championship,' was his pointed remark. Indeed, Ferrari didn't seem at all happy. Gearbox and engine problems had hampered Mansell in practice and Prost had laboured hard to no sensational outcome.

On the grid, Benetton were reasonably placed especially for a circuit where some drivers contend that it is easier to win from the back. Piquet was on the third row, Nannini back on the eleventh, but it was the new French star, Jean Alesi, in the Pirelli-shod Tyrrell who scythed around the front of the grid to streak away in the lead.

He was going great guns and was soon some 10 seconds ahead. Behind him the Dodgem Syndrome was taking its toll. The veteran Italian, Riccardo Patrese, lost the nose cone of his Williams and had to come in for repairs. Larini, some ten years younger than his countryman, bounced his Ligier into a barrier and walked away furious with himself. Piquet's Benetton was running smoothly in sixth place and then the flying Berger overcooked it on a bend and slid into a barrier constructed of old tyres. The Austrian tried frantically to drive his car away from the tyres but they reached out to enfold him like the tentacles of an octopus – and that was one McLaren out of contention.

Lap 9 and Piquet was in fourth place with Alesi still in front. Berger was back in the race no doubt wishing that he could have emulated one of the super-heroes of old film serials –

Nannini relaxing during the Estoril tyre tests.

Nannini relaxing again — this time over a quiet game of cards.

'One bound and he was free' – in escaping from the clutches of those damn tyres. Piquet, unperturbed, went his steady way. By lap 15 the Benetton driver was still holding on to fourth place and shortly afterwards he moved up briefly to third.

Alesi, in only his ninth Grand Prix, was still the leader but his lead was gradually being whittled away by – who else? – Ayrton Senna. The Frenchman now had a margin of 5.2 seconds, half what it had been at one stage. Prost's Ferrari had been spraying oil from the rear-end for some time and now the World Champion disappeared into the pits. By lap 23 the order was Alesi, Senna, Piquet. Andrea de Cesaris (Dallara) went out when in fifth position. The Italian charger, labelled 'de Crasheris' by one correspondent, had been driving well.

After 34 laps Alesi was still ahead, just, but the race was about to reach its climax. The next two laps saw an exciting battle for the leadership – and ultimate victory. Senna was hustling and harrying the Tyrrell driver and eventually got through. Whether or not the Brazilian felt that was it and Alesi was now a spent force who can tell? But Senna let the McLaren swing out and immediately Alesi cut in to pass him and take the lead once more. Next time around it started to happen again: Senna passed Alesi and this time when the Frenchman mounted his counterattack Senna had closed the gap. There was no way through.

The second half of the race was something of an anti-climax after that. Another driver once associated with the Benetton story, Thierry Boutsen, had steadily moved up the field in one of the Williams and Piquet was back in fourth place where he had been most of the race. The order of the cars now was Senna, Alesi, Boutsen, Piquet.

Nelson Piquet in action during the 1990 US Grand Prix at Phoenix, Arizona.

Piquet under pressure at Phoenix.

It looked as if there might still be some real excitement as Nigel Mansell came charging through the field in his Ferrari. He was in fifth place and threatening Piquet when oil blew out over his rear tyres, there was a sheet of flame, the car spun and the Englishman's race was run. Doubtless, there were also some heated exchanges in the Ferrari pits.

So the order remained unchanged with three laps to go and only fourteen of the original twenty-six starters still running. No one took any chances in the closing minutes and the scoring six were:

1. Ayrton Senna (McLaren)
2. Jean Alesi (Tyrrell)
3. Thierry Boutsen (Williams)
4. Nelson Piquet (Benetton)
5. Stefano Modena (Brabham)
6. Satoru Nakajima (Tyrrell)

A surprising-looking scoreboard to anyone who had been following the varied prognostications of motoring correspondents, team chiefs, sponsors and Joe Soap in the corner with his thumb in his mouth. At least four of the six were totally unexpected. Nelson Piquet had already been written-off by the majority, a three-times World Champion who no longer had the will to win, so they said. And, although Alesi had been hailed as the brightest of the rising stars in 1989, no one had contemplated two Tyrrells in

157

Cars dwarfed by the skyscrapers of Phoenix. The car in the foreground is Piquet's Benetton.

The minnows: Oscar Larrauri, Argentinian driver, who has been with Eurobrun in Formula 1 and sports cars since 1985.

the first six let alone one of them leading for nearly half the race.

The biggest surprise of the lot was Modena, the Italian from Modena, in fifth place in a Brabham. Brabham have had ownership difficulties and right up to the last moment it wasn't certain that they would be able to race at Phoenix – or at all in 1990.

All in all, the United States Grand Prix must have given most teams some ground for encouragement in the 1990s. The minnows like Minardi, Eurobrun, Dallara, Osella, Lola and Brabham all had moments when the blood was stirred and the cause did not look completely hopeless. Williams showed once again that should McLaren slip they will be around to take advantage.

Only Ferrari looked to be in trouble at this point and no one would write them off too easily. The Italian team has been in crisis situations before and always they come back to pose a threat to the best.

The minnows: Erich Zakowski with his Zakspeed car dropped out in the nineties. Jonathan Palmer was one of the drivers who persevered with the Zakspeed.

Alessandro Nannini at Phoenix.

For the Benetton and Ford partnership the future remained full of promise. Piquet's fourth place was a fair return from a 'lottery' apart from settling any doubts there might have been about the driver's ability and with a new additional sponsor, Nippon Autopolis (a Japanese commercial property development consortium), looking on it was a pleasing result with which to head for Brazil and the next race. Especially as improved chassis and improved engines were in the pipeline.

Yet over all was the brooding shadow of Ayrton Senna and McLaren. Driver extraordinaire. Car extraordinaire. It very much looked as if Benetton or anyone else who wanted to be Grand Prix king in the coming decade had first to find the answer to the Brazilian's supreme artistry behind the wheel. But there were many races yet to come. In fact it was . . .

One Down and One Hundred and Fifty-Nine to Come . . .

Benetton Ford at Silverstone in 1990: note the new sponsor Autopolis has been added to the list.

Another view of the car at Silverstone.

Benetton and Ford came away from Arizona with their faith in a good 1990 season unimpaired. Nelson Piquet, Gordon Message, Michael Kranefuss, Dick Scammell – all felt that the first 'adventure' of the racing year had been a good one for the Witney-based equipe.

Piquet is not too keen on street circuits and so his third row of the grid, fourth place in the race, was actually a greater achievement than it might seem on paper. Apart from one or two minor matters he was pleased with both car and engine.

Nannini was unlucky. He had a misfire and a disastrous twenty-second best time in the first qualifying session, rain in the second which prevented him moving up the grid, and two pit stops in the race itself – one to change a broken rear wheel on the first lap and the other to change a front wing after running over some debris on the track. To finish 11th after all that was yet another indication that the Benettons were very much to be reckoned with at their present state of development.

The backroom boys were pretty much agreed in their assessment of the situation.

Michael Kranefuss said:

'With three Ford engines finishing in the points, we have started 1990 on a high note. [The other two Ford engines were in the Tyrrells of Alesi and Nakajima – Author.] It was good to see Nelson slotting into the Benneton Ford team so effectively and just as satisfying to have a trouble-free run with the car and engine on what is a difficult street circuit. We are looking forward to a good season.'

Cosworth's Dick Scammell was just as chirpy:

'The new third-generation Ford V8 performed well at Phoenix and although it revs higher and produces more power, Nelson Piquet expressed himself pleased with its driveability. We will have nine engines available for the Benetton Ford team in Brazil and look forward to a good race result. Looking back at the Phoenix results it

was good to see how well the Ford DFRs performed, taking second and sixth places.'

If Dick's pleasure was a little diminished by the fact that his 'reserve' engines had beaten his 'first team' he didn't show it.

Gordon Message was a little more guarded in his remarks. Grand Prix team managers are a little bit like football team managers. If things are not going too well, the team manager's head is usually the one most accessible for the chopping block. And these days the executioners don't often bother to say 'thank you'.

Gordon was optimistic, nevertheless. With the next race scheduled for Brazil he thought the circuit would suit them better than

Michael Kranefuss at work.

Phoenix, he was pleased with the performance of the engine and liked the revised aero-dynamics of the car. Not that anyone could be certain about the circuit. It was at Interlagos true, but the circuit had been greatly modified since it was last used for Grand Prix racing in 1980. Although using parts of the old circuit, the new one was shorter but also had two straights which ought to be of help to those with the most powerful power-plants.

From a detached observer's point of view Interlagos had two things going in its favour in so far as Benetton was concerned. The obvious one was that the circuit should give Piquet and Nannini the chance to make maximum use of the power available to them. The other was that the Benetton Ford team still did not have the burden of media pressure full on them.

The up-and-coming young French driver, Alesi (Tyrrell); Nigel Mansell and another dramatic exit from a race; the McLaren–Ferrari–Williams battle; the revived tyre battle between Pirelli and Goodyear: these were the topics monopolising the press coverage as 25 March and the Brazilian Grand Prix drew near.

Out-and-out favourite was Ayrton Senna, of course. The Brazilian ace had won the US Grand Prix. Now he was coming home, the king about to claim his throne, and there was no doubt that the crowd would be cheering for the man they regarded as the greatest race driver in the world. You can read what you like into history, statistics and the law of averages and invariably come up with facts and figures for whatever line of reasoning you want to pursue.

Since 1972 (which was a non-championship race) the Brazilian Grand Prix had been run 18 times and had been won 9 times by South American drivers: Carlos Reutemann (four), Emerson Fittipaldi and Nelson Piquet (twice each) and Carlos Pace (once). That seemed to make Senna an even chance, and on his current form an odds-on favourite.

There is always a 'but' however. Since 1982, the race had gone to Alain Prost (five times), Nelson Piquet (twice) and Nigel Mansell who

Emerson Fittipaldi, Indy 500 winner, who like Nelson Piquet, has won the Brazilian Grand Prix twice.

was the 1989 winner when Senna finished 11th. Prost, Piquet and Mansell would all be competing against Senna in the 1990 event and on that basis, Senna did not seem such a sure thing.

So it proved . . .

70,000 passionate fans packed the circuit, now named after the popular but ill-fated Carlos Pace, winner of the Brazilian Grand Prix in 1975, and it is a fair bet that most of them wanted Senna to win.

For a mighty long while it appeared that their idol *would* win his native Grand Prix for the first time but the pack was always snarling on his heels and when misfortune struck the Brazilian he had no time left to recover. The physical damage was – once again – to the nose cone and front wing of Senna's McLaren and this time it happened as he attempted to overtake Japan's

163

No. 1 driver, Satoru Nakajima (Tyrrell). The time subsequently spent in the pits effectively robbed Senna of any chance of victory. 'I knew I could not catch up so I just settled for third place,' he said afterwards.

Brazil may be the place where the nuts come form but for Alain Prost they come gold-plated. He went on to win his first race for Ferrari, his sixth Brazilian Grand Prix and his fortieth Grand Prix in all and, presumably, had the satisfaction of taking a prize from the man with whom he had feuded for most of the previous season.

One detected also a note of relief in Prost's remarks after the laurel wreath had surmounted his shoulders:

'I am very pleased because we had a difficult time at Phoenix and afterwards. It is not always easy to work for Ferrari where you have to explain everything that goes wrong.'

The circuit was bathed in sunshine when the race started in what had become almost customary fashion with Senna streaking away into the lead from pole position, pursued by Boutsen (Williams), Prost (Ferrari), Berger (McLaren), Mansell (Ferrari) and Patrese (Williams). Behind them the well-known crash artiste, Andrea de Cesaris (Dallara) had a collision and ran off at the first corner.

Mansell was once again in trouble and had to make a pit stop after 27 laps when he was in sixth place. Like Queen Victoria, he was not much amused.

Prost was running second to Senna and after the latter's coming together with Nakajima, the little Frenchman took over the lead and stayed out in front for the rest of the race, some 30 of the 71 laps. 'It was a fantastic day and a fantastic win for me and the team.'

Which is more than former Witney drivers now with Team Camel Lotus could say. Derek Warwick had to retire through electrical troubles while Martin Donnelly spun off after 43 laps.

The incumbent Benetton tenants had better but mixed luck. Piquet once again drove with cool and steady hands, bringing his car home in sixth place and earning a point which might or might not help out the finances at the end of the season.

Piquet in the Brazilian Grand Prix at Interlagos.

Nannini cornering in the Brazilian Grand Prix, 1990.

Close-up of Piquet in the 1990 Brazilian Grand Prix.

The luckless Sandro Nannini was once again involved in a first-lap incident which sent him into the pits early in the action. Then, after he got back into the race, he suffered a puncture with just a few laps to go which meant a dismal start to a season which had promised much after the encouraging results towards the close of the 1989 campaign. But it was early days yet and Sandro consoled himself that the next race would be in his native land.

So this time the six scoring positions were as follows:

1. Alain Prost (Ferrari)
2. Gerhard Berger (McLaren)
3. Ayrton Senna (McLaren)
4. Nigel Mansell (Ferrari)
5. Thierry Boutsen (Williams)
6. Nelson Piquet (Benetton)

There were big celebrations in the Ferrari garage not surprisingly since the team had claimed first and fourth places after both cars had failed to finish in Phoenix and Berger too had great satisfaction after claiming his first points since joining the McLaren team in place of Prost. And who can blame the veteran Piquet if he permitted himself a quiet little chuckle for snatching sixth place after passing the bright new talent, Jean Alesi, on the last lap but one? So now it was . . .

Two Down and One Hundred and Fifty-Eight to Come . . .

Nannini at Interlagos.

The Phoenix and Sao Paulo Grands Prix were what the television moguls would call a mini-series since after their completion there was a seven-week lull in the schedule before the Grand Prix programme recommenced. 'Lull' is used advisedly since for most teams it was a period of frantic work – on cars, engines and in some cases, drivers, injured, sick or just not good enough.

For Gordon Message and his team it meant bedding-in the new B190 car, complete with revised V8. Testing was done at Imola, venue of the next Grand Prix, the San Marino, and although the weather was poor, Gordon saw enough to feel that the prospects were exciting. He said:

'Despite the weather we were able to do some constructive running and, in my view, the times achieved showed considerable promise. The B190 has greater aerodynamic efficiency than the B189 and perhaps just as important is much more driver-friendly than the predecessor.'

Driver-friendly. Two words which teams may have to pay more and more attention to in the future. There has been a tendency in modern racing to concentrate on car and engine design and not give too much thought to the driver other than measuring his vital statistics and allowing just enough space in the cockpit for him. As mentioned earlier, life has become almost impossible for bigger men such as Eddie Cheever and drivers like Nigel Mansell and Sandro Nannini have finished in a state of exhaustion several times. If they were otters, the animal rights people would be after Ballestre, Ecclestone & Co.!

Reverting to Benetton Ford, Gordon's hopes were echoed by Dick Scammell who said that the engine had been further revised since the Brazilian Grand Prix and shown up well during testing at Imola. And Gordon came back to point out that Piquet and Nannini had been lapping within a couple of tenths of a second of each other, and that Nannini had been third at Imola the previous year and would be determined to do his best on Italian soil.

'All we need is for his luck to change.'

Again there wasn't too much press attention on the Benetton Ford combo. 'Mansell's Target', 'Stunning Senna', 'Senna's Practice Perfection', 'Ferrari Set Up Takeover Bid' — and that was just the British press. The Italian media, with daggers dipped in Borgia poison and minds cultivated on the machinations of Machiavelli, had more private fights allegedly going on between Ferrari, McLaren, Williams, Prost, Senna, Mansell and Japan for good measure, than Casanova had girl-friends. And if Franco Lini or Charles Riccono, to name but two, ever read this may they forgive me.

Amidst the commotion it almost escaped notice that another Brabham had appeared on the scene, this time Sir Jack's youngest, David, British Formula 3 Champion and winner of the Macau Formula 3 Grand Prix.

Unlike 28-year-old sibling Gary (entered earlier in the season by the Life team), 24-year-old David was down to drive a Brabham, which must have brought back some memories for Jack.

This was too human a story for most of the tabloids who concentrated on the more ghoulish aspects of the imagined feelings of Austrian driver Gerhard Berger who survived a 'flamer' in the previous year's race and now had to go out and race again through that selfsame corner. Berger did confess to some tremors (who wouldn't?) but still managed to put it far enough behind him as to qualify on the front row.

Indeed, the qualifying process was as exciting as for many races. The rivalry in the McLaren team between Senna and Berger may not have been as intense as that between Senna and Prost the previous year but you would not have known it by the duel fought by these two to decide pole position on the grid. When it was all over and Senna had beaten his team-mate's brilliant early lap by just one half-second, the Brazilian made sure no one could misunderstand the position by saying, 'When you have a team-mate you admire and respect it gives you the extra motivation.'

Mansell was disappointed but not deterred by fifth place on the grid with the Williams' duo, Patrese and Boutsen, heading him and his team-mate, and the reigning world champion, Prost, following on.

Although Mansell felt he had no chance of catching the McLaren pair in qualifying, he did feel that he could have been third on the grid, if given a clear lap in qualifying. As it was he had a couple of 'happenings' apart from cluttered tracks. In one case he went over the kerb and in the other he went straight on at the chicane when his foot wedged between brake pedal and throttle. He was still a very confident racer and felt that the Ferraris were in with a real chance.

Benetton were not saying very much at all but there was a suspicion of satisfaction on Gordon Message's countenance. Piquet was in eighth place on the grid, Nannini in seventh, and both were obviously in contention.

The Arrows, Alboreto and Caffi, failed to qualify. So, alas, did David Brabham. The one on whom the gods smiled was our old friend Pierluigi Martini who crashed in his Minardi during the opening qualifying session. He escaped with nothing worse than a chipped heel-bone and a few minor injuries.

The race itself was an exciting one and kept up the 1990 pattern of a different winner for each race. Maybe Benetton Ford hopes were not entirely realised but they were far from dashed. Nannini at last had his share of whatever luck was going and repeated his 1989 performance by coming in third. His team-mate Piquet finished fifth, his third successive race in the points.

The headlines however were again centred upon Nigel Mansell and his erstwhile chum and team-mate Gerhard Berger. Not that either of them won the race, indeed Mansell did not even finish it.

The story unfolded thus . . .

For once Senna played no major role despite being in pole position for the sixth time at Imola and the forty-fourth time in his career. His right rear tyre punctured on lap 4 and that was the end of matters as far as the Brazilian was concerned. The race settled into a battle royal between Mansell, roared on by the Italian crowd to whom he has become a hero during his sojourn with Ferrari, and Gerhard Berger, himself with Ferrari last season and now taking Prost's place in the McLaren team.

There are at least three versions of what took place between the two on lap 36 of the 61-lap race.

Drily factual news agency reports said that Mansell went into a full 360-degree spin when he attempted to pass Berger and take the lead. The Austrian, they said, closed the door on him as he tried to squeeze past. Mansell was not quite so cool about the affair. Said he:

'I have never been so disappointed or upset as I am now. Gerhard is a friend of mine and I can't believe what he did. It was my race. He was pushing me off the circuit and he wasn't even subtle about it. Everyone saw it. I don't think it was very professional and I cannot understand it.'

Berger insisted:

'In no way was it deliberate. It was tough for me in the lead at that time and I realised that if I made a mistake I would be in big trouble. I knew Nigel was behind me going into the corner and would be looking to overtake me soon. I saw him in my mirror, saw his nose cone on my left and started to move back to the racing line but then he went onto the grass. I was sorry about it. I don't like things like that to happen. I know it's a dangerous place and I don't like it.'

Summation of views amongst the circuit rail dog birds inclined to a theory along these lines: Berger was expecting Mansell to launch his attack at the end of the straight rather than on the exit of the very fast Tamburello curve. He was surprised when Mansell made an early move but, by the same token the Englishman was equally surprised when Berger moved on to the racing line which Mansell thought he had a claim to having signalled his intentions by pulling out of the McLaren's slipstream. When the Austrian flicked his car into the path of the Ferrari, Mansell had no option but to take to the grass.

Fortunately, his car lurched back on to the tarmac in a cloud of smoke coming from the screaming tyres. Mansell carried on in his usual charging fashion but three laps later his engine expired and he had to retire. 'My car was performing all right after the spin and I wasn't aware of any problems until I had to come into the pits.'

When you realise that all this took place at something around 195mph (315kph) it is not surprising that verbal exchanges were somewhat heated, but the general opinion seemed to be that it was a genuine misunderstanding between two fine drivers, one of those things which is bound to happen from time to time in a high-speed sport.

After finishing the race, Gerhard Berger extended his apologies but by that time Mansell, who had to have some stitches in a wound sustained in the paddock before the race, was already heading away from the circuit in his helicopter *en route* to his home in the Isle of Man.

There was disappointment for Berger too since another challenger would replace Mansell and this one would be successful.

1990 had thus far been a year for the sporting underdogs and the San Marino Grand Prix was no exception. 36-year-old Riccardo Patrese was not only one of the oldest drivers on the circuit but one of the most experienced, having driven in 195 Grands Prix prior to Imola. He had often been in the headlines (usually for the wrong reasons, as mentioned earlier) and in all those 195 starts he had only assumed the mantle of victor on two occasions. There had nearly been a third – at Imola in 1983 when he lost the race with four laps to go, crashing into a tyre wall with the race in his

pocket. It hurt – and so did the cheers of the crowd who apparently preferred seeing a foreign driver win in an Italian car to an Italian driver winning in a foreign car. Patrese never rid himself of the memories of that day, his own mistake and the way his countrymen rejoiced in his downfall. Imola, 1990, gave him the opportunity of erasing the bad and substituting a happier memory.

His Williams was away to a poor start but after that Patrese settled down. The aim was to drive steadily, conserve rubber and then be prepared to make a challenge in the closing stages. He carried out the plan to the letter and few would have recognised him as the reckless driver of yesteryear. With Mansell's retirement Patrese found himself in second place and was soon on the McLaren's heels.

With ten laps to go, Patrese passed Berger and took a lead which he was never to relinquish. 'I was crying all round the last lap' he said. And the Italian crowd, for once, forbore to jeer.

Meanwhile life was interesting for the Benetton boys, with the spotlight more on Nannini than Piquet. Sandro was going well during first practice until a coming together with the BSM Dallara of the ubiquitous Master de Cesaris which ended with Nannini going off and badly damaging the chassis of his car. With a few well-chosen words on the subject of certain people, Sandro went out in the spare car and was tenth fastest overnight. Piquet meanwhile had been minding his own business and at that stage was eighth fastest. Times were naturally faster at Saturday practice but Nelson hung on to eighth place while his team-mate managed to move up to seventh.

In the race itself, Piquet was in collision early on with Jean Alesi and thereafter had some trouble with his steering. However, he kept going steadily for his third points finish in three races.

Nannini had his own battles to wage, principally with Alain Prost. Their struggle enlivened the later stages of the race, Nannini eventually prevailing to gain third spot, less than a second ahead of the Frenchman.

In the heat of the moment afterwards, Sandro uttered some words which brought press criticism down on his head, words which in the cold light of the next day he may have wished he had never uttered.

Pointing out that at one stage he had a comfortable 10-second advantage over Prost, he went on to attack the Lotus pair, Warwick and Donnelly, for holding him up and enabling Prost to catch up again. Warwick and Donnelly were fighting for places at the time (they were eventually classified seventh and eighth) and general opinion seemed to be that there was no call for Nannini to describe them both as 'stupid'. On the other hand, it is perhaps too much to hope these days that racing-drivers should be any different to soccer and rugger players, cricketers or snooker players. Shout, swear and if that still doesn't relieve your feelings, belt 'em.

Thus the race ended:

1. Riccardo Patrese (Williams)
2. Gerhard Berger (McLaren)
3. Alessandro Nannini (Benetton)
4. Alain Prost (Ferrari)
5. Nelson Piquet (Benetton)
6. Jean Alesi (Tyrrell)

Nannini had the consolation of setting fastest lap on the penultimate lap of the race. Ford and Cosworth had the pleasure of three Ford engines in the first six, Alesi's DFR being the third.

And Piquet was now equal sixth in the Drivers' Championship, tied with Thierry Boutsen. Nannini was right behind them in eighth slot. Senna (thirteenth) led from Prost and Berger (twelfth equal) and Patrese (ninth). Interesting that of the top eight drivers, no less than six were present or former Toleman/Benetton men.

The race left Benetton in fourth place in the Constructors' Championship. McLaren-Honda were out in front as usual with 25 points and then came Ferrari and Williams-Renault with 15 each. Benetton-Ford had 10 points and were followed by Tyrrell-Ford DFR with 8 points and Brabham-Judd with 2 points. At least there were indications that the era of utter McLaren domination was coming to a close, something which in the long term and the short, could only be good for the sport as a whole. But McLaren were certainly not finished, not by a long way.

When all the angry comments had evaporated, when the last spectator had gone and the last scribe had packed his fax machine, the heat and sunshine of Imola but a memory, the situation now was . . .

Three Down and One Hundred and Fifty-Seven to Come . . .

Benetton Ford had reason to think that the power situation was coming along nicely. Nannini's fastest lap at Imola was 129.27mph (208.03kph) against the lap record of 129.89mph (209.03kph) held by Prost in a McLaren. The next race on the schedule, however, was Monaco, a race for the streetwise where sheer power did not count for everything. Even so the Witney team could feel that this was a season which had started off very well for them.

Chief Designer Rory Byrne was pleased with the new B190.

'It was an encouraging début especially as we started eighth and ninth on the grid. The result would have been even better if Nelson hadn't had a coming together with Alesi's Tyrrell. His car was thrown into the air and the rear suspension was damaged, making steering difficult. Nelson showed tremendous determination to bring his car home in the points and the way Sandro held off the challenge from Prost in the latter stages was most impressive. There's no doubt we have a really good combination of drivers.'

A 1990 portrait of Nelson Piquet . . .

. . . and Piquet in action.

Benetton 'brains', John Barnard and Rory Byrne.

John Barnard and Nelson Piquet.

Cosworth's Dick Scammell was just as enthusiastic.

Phoenix had demonstrated that the Ford engine had good driveability and Imola that it was competitive in the new chassis. Now Cosworth and Ford Electronics were getting their heads together to see what improvements could be made.

Benetton and Ford continued to be a partnership which seemed destined for the top. . .

Monaco is the most crowded country in Europe (36,000 people per sq mile, or 14,000 per sq km, at the last count) and at least 100,000 more descend upon the little principality for the Grand Prix which is still the most glamorous, famous and unusual in the world.

Monte Carlo is a city which has a reputation all of its own, one of a handful in the world which in their varying ways have a mystique which no one can quite analyse and yet which holds millions in thrall and enthralled. Paris, Las

Money is the name of the game in Monte Carlo despite the fact that it's more than 100 years since someone broke the bank at the casino (an Englishman named Charles Wells in 1887). In 1990, £500 was being quoted as the asking price for a modest hotel room, and champagne was being flogged at £60 a bottle. For £10,000, a balcony could be hired; a dolphin's eye-view from the yachts in the harbour cost considerably more. But the champagne and lobsters came at no extra charge. Much was made in the public prints of a handful of drivers earning £6 million (or $6 million?) or more for the season – but then they were risking their necks, not their digestion.

Benetton director Flavio Briatore and John Barnard.

Vegas, New Orleans, Vienna . . . there aren't too many of them. Monte Carlo is the archetype. Its casino, setting for myriad films, stage plays and television productions; the song, 'The Man Who Broke the Bank at Monte Carlo', dating back to the days of Victorian music hall; a ruler with a fabulous collection of veteran, vintage and classic cars and whose late consort, Grace Kelly, was one of Hollywood's most beautiful stars; some of the plushest hotels in the world and a harbour crowded with the yachts and cruisers of the wealthy, the famous, those with 'mega-bucks' and those with ideas on how to part them from their mega-bucks.

During race week everyone who has a boat in the harbour can rely on a maximum number of guests, invited or uninvited. The hotels, expensive as they are, are booked to the hilt. Rich men and joyful young fillies abound. Race followers of more modest means often find it better to stay outside Monaco and commute to practices and the race. There are excellent rail and bus services to and from Monte Carlo to Nice and other places along the coast. But come race day they will all be there – clinging on to the hillside, packing every window and doorway . . . who wants to miss the Monaco Grand Prix?

The answer to that question might well be: some of the drivers. With the blinding speed of today's Grand Prix cars, Monaco has become something of an anachronism, the narrow streets making overtaking extremely difficult as well as highly dangerous and the cars often only inches from the barriers. It puts a premium on qualifying well. A driver on pole position, getting away in the lead, can stay out in front providing his car and engine don't let him down. Fortunately, or unfortunately according to your point of view, the field is usually greatly reduced by the time the chequered flag is due. In other words, tail-enders on the grid who manage to keep going can often end up in the points simply by default.

Benetton, although not dissatisfied with the way the season had commenced, would not

Backroom boys get more tense than drivers – Nelson Piquet gives John Barnard a shoulder massage.

vote the principality as their favourite motor-racing venue. Ferrari probably felt much the same way. Mansell is said not to like Monaco although his team-mate Prost has won here four times and on this occasion would be bidding to equal Graham Hill's record of five wins.

By and large the newspapers were in agreement in the days leading up to the race (the motoring correspondents and not the gossip columnists, that is): 'Senna is streets ahead of the field' read one headline. 'Alesi's street cred grows,' said another. 'Alesi tipped by the master' said a third. In case, you dear reader, would like to know, 'the master' referred to in this case was Alain Prost.

For once it seemed the pundits could be right. Senna was soon showing his stuff. In the

Monaco is the one Grand Prix where the British press attach more importance to sending their gossip columnists rather than their motoring correspondents. They report on one-time playboy Dai Llewellyn, son of Colonel Harry of 'Foxhunter' show jumping fame, collecting cash for Telethon . . . on British footballers Mark Hately and Glenn Hoddle, who both play for the local French league club, driving BMWs and lazing in the sun . . . on Prince Rainier's sons-in-law, present and to come . . . and on the Greek shipping billionaire, Stavros Niarchos, and the size of his yacht. One columnist forgot himself so much as to mention motor racing and Benetton's Nelson Piquet, but only to calculate the number of the Brazilian's girl-friends and children . . .

first qualifying session he knocked a half-second off his pole-earning time of the previous year, then came in to issue the chilling warning, 'I can go faster still.'

Yet if there was going to be a surprise, the inexperienced Frenchman, Jean Alesi, was the man most likely to spring it. In only his second Grand Prix season he was impressing all the experts. In 1989 he had had six Formula 1 drives and collected 8 points. Thus far in 1990 his three drives had brought him 7 points. Also in his favour was the fact that he had done well on another street circuit, Phoenix, and that winning at Monaco had been a dream since he had first spectated there as a teenager back in 1983.

An aggressive driver ('a certain arrogance, which is not a bad thing,' says his entrant Ken Tyrrell), the 26-year-old Frenchman believes it is important for other drivers to see how competitive he is. It seems unlikely that any of them are under any misapprehensions about that.

Harvey Postlethwaite, Tyrrell designer by way of Hesketh and Ferrari, thinks there is a more simple explanation for Alesi's success thus far: 'He isn't sitting on a pile of gold and he hasn't got 15 kids.'

As if in confirmation of that prognosis, the acknowledged Monaco specialist, Prost, said Monaco belonged to the past. 'It's not safe and

each year it gets worse for me.' Then added ruefully, 'It must be my age.'

The reigning World Champion may believe what he says or may wish to lull his adversaries into a state of false hope. The fact remains that when all practising and qualifying was over he was on the front row of the grid right alongside his old team-mate and adversary, Senna.

He was struggling for a while in the first qualifying session but eventually found the moment to put in a lap which lifted him to fourth place on the grid. In final qualifying he had, unusually for him, a spin which caused a little damage to the car's rear end, but went out later to do a time which put him second on the grid. Yet there were no fireworks, nothing spectacular – just a neat and tidy drive, always on the correct line and never wasting a moment. Some others would like to be so old and so afraid . . .

However, just as in the race proper, it is essential not to get baulked by slower movers in order to record a fast qualifying time. Nigel Mansell, never overwhelmed in admiration for the circuit, had trouble throughout qualifying and eventually made seventh position. Even Senna, trying to improve on his time, had trouble when the Swiss driver Gregor Foitek, who had switched to Montiverdi Onyx-Ford from Brabham, wandered across his path. Alesi was not too happy either – Prost having robbed him of the front row position he had his heart on.

The happiest driver on the circuit was David Brabham (Brabham) who, by making twenty-fifth place out of twenty-six, qualified for his first Grand Prix start. It meant he would be racing at Monaco whilst his elder brother, Geoff, would be competing in the fabulous Indianapolis 500 on the same day.

Benetton found themselves in a sort of no man's land. Sandro Nannini had problems right from the start and eventually qualified way down the field. Nelson Piquet, who calls Monte Carlo home, did rather better and qualified in tenth place, a position which gave him a good chance of finishing in the points for the fourth successive race.

Probably happier were two Benetton 'old boys' making their Monaco débuts. Emanuele Pirro, who had a half-season with the Witney team, qualified his Dallara-Ford in ninth place whilst Martin Donnelly, who had tried out with Benetton, made it to eleventh, a couple of places ahead of his team-mate, that well-known Toleman 'old boy', Derek Warwick, a man with a self-confessed liking for the tricky Monte Carlo circuit.

Patrese (Williams) was fourth, Berger (McLaren) fifth, Boutsen (Williams) sixth, Martini (Minardi-Ford) eighth – a bit of a surprise, this – de Cesaris (Dallara-Ford) twelfth, Modena (Brabham-Judd) fourteenth and Suzuki (Larrousse-Lamborghini) fifteenth. The remaining eleven were reckoned to have no chance – but at Monaco who can tell?

Nannini, in sixteenth place, must certainly have been hoping for miracles. Behind him were Larini (Ligier), Alliot (Ligier), Barilla (Minardi), Foitek (Onyx), Nakajima (Tyrrell), Caffi (Arrows), Capelli (Leyton House), Bernard (Lola), D. Brabham (Brabham) and Lehto (Onyx).

The fierce competition which is modern Grand Prix racing meant that four good drivers, one of them very good, were left to spectate – Michele Alboreto (Arrows), Olivier Grouillard (Osella) and the two Brazilians, Maurice Gugelmin (Leyton House) and Robert Moreno (Eurobrun).

The dramas began almost as the start lights went on . . .

Nannini was having trouble after just a few hundred yards, flames were coming from the rear end of Capelli's car . . . and the mud-pies really hit the fan when Berger tried to follow Alesi past Prost on the inside – and found the hole wasn't there. A wheel sheered off the Austrian's car in the most spectacular fashion and with all the cars locked together in a jam which would not have disgraced the Brighton road on a bank holiday, the race was ordered to re-start.

It meant a brisk run back to the pits for Berger and Prost to get the spare cars, and un-

fortunately for both, each team had the car set up for the other driver. In other words the spare McLaren was set up for Senna and the spare Ferrari for Mansell. It meant more difficulty for Berger than for Prost. Prost is a small man but Berger is a biggish fellow who has difficulty getting into the cockpit anyway. According to James Hunt, McLaren had worked during the winter with Berger using a car which did not meet the new pedal regulations. When the Grand Prix season started, the Austrian had to be crammed into a regulation car. Now he was going to try and race in one with even less room. The McLaren pit – and the Ferrari one – made possible last-minute adjustments and the rest was in the lap of the gods.

Hunt had the last word: 'If you pay a driver five million dollars a year it seems silly not to have a car which fits him.' Under the circumstances Berger's subsequent drive tinges on the heroic.

A familiar picture emerged when the race re-started: Senna in the lead, Prost second – and the speeds around 87mph (140kph) which is fast for this circuit of 3,000 gearshifts.

Senna was building a comfortable lead and was 8.7 sec ahead of Prost who in turn was only 1.2 sec in front of the marauding Alesi.

Larini had gone out but all the main contenders were still there. Boutsen was sixth, Mansell seventh and Piquet, giving rise to Benetton hopes, eighth. Nannini too had moved up the field and was eleventh.

David Brabham's first Grand Prix came to a summary end and Mansell had to pit for repairs to a front wing, his tyres being changed at the same time.

Twenty-five laps gone and Piquet was in seventh place but a long way behind him Mansell was setting a new lap record as he tried to get back into contention.

Senna posted a new record and the order now was Senna, Prost, Alesi, Berger, Patrese, Boutsen, Piquet, de Cesaris and Warwick. But not for long. Prost went into the pits and retired.

There was a real glow now in the Benetton pit. Piquet was in sixth place. Could he finish in the points for the fourth time in four starts? He was the only hope now – Nannini's car having been brought back ignominiously by a break-down truck.

It was not to be. Piquet spun and lost part of his frontage. He had to be pushed to re-start and so was automatically out of the race. He jumped to no conclusions. After repairs he poked his nose out on to the circuit again but was promptly black-flagged by the marshals so his race was done.

Barilla spun, Nakajima went into the pits and by the time the race had got to lap 39 the order was Senna, Alesi, Berger, Patrese, Boutsen, Warwick.

Patrese went into the pits and Warwick was up into fifth place with Mansell, who had been gobbling up the opposition since he was forced to stop, now in sixth position. Mansell then overtook Warwick and, meanwhile, Patrese, who had resumed after his pit-stop, went back into the pits, this time for good.

With two-thirds of the race completed, Senna was 23 sec ahead of Alesi, his nearest rival, but the fiery Mansell had moved up into fourth place.

Senna was amusing himself breaking lap records and only nine cars were now left of the original twenty-six.

Mansell's heroic drive came to an end with fifteen laps to go – his Ferrari developing gearbox trouble. Nigel managed a half-hearted wave to his supporters as he walked back to the pits but was undoubtedly seething inside. It had been a magnificent performance but once again had ended in disappointment.

Eight left and soon there were only seven. Derek Warwick, with a first-of-the-season points tally almost a certainty, spun and stalled and had to be craned off the circuit. Brake fading was the cause. The incident might have cost Senna the race. He came around the corner to be confronted by Warwick's Lotus which was slewed across the track and did well to avoid it.

The seven now remaining were Senna, Alesi, Berger, Boutsen, Caffi – a welcome break for the disappointing and disappointed Arrows – Foitek and Bernard. And unusually in a motor race there were two thrilling battles in the closing stages. One was between Alesi and Berger for second place, the other – and perhaps even more fiercely fought – was between Foitek and Bernard, the latter suddenly seeing the prospect of avoiding pre-qualifying in future if he could finish in the first six ahead of Foitek.

And finish sixth he did, Foitek being tailed off some six laps behind and the last of the entrants to be classified. The struggle up front had some added zest when Senna suddenly slowed, but he had so much in hand that there was never really any danger of him being caught, although as Alesi and Berger closed up the crowd were given an unexpected thrill.

Thus the scoring six were:

1. Ayrton Senna (McLaren-Honda)
2. Jean Alesi (Tyrrell-Ford)
3. Gerhard Berger (McLaren-Honda)
4. Thierry Boutsen (Williams-Renault)
5. Alex Caffi (Arrows-Ford)
6. Eric Bernard (Larrousse-Lamborghini)

Senna, of course, had driven brilliantly again and because he so often gets out in front and stays there, one wonders if he is not given the credit that is his due. As it was, the accolades for the 1990 Monaco Grand Prix seemed to go to Berger, for an undoubtedly heroic drive in a strange car, and Mansell for being out of luck again after an all-out charge which brought him up from the tail of the field (sixteenth) to fourth place.

Yet, at the end of the day, one hard fact could not be denied – Senna had won again and was now comfortably in the lead for the Drivers' Championship, which at this stage of the season read:

1. Ayrton Senna (Brazil)   22 points
2. Gerhard Berger (Austria)   16

3.	Jean Alesi (France)	13	1.	McLaren-Honda	38 points
4.	Alain Prost (France)	12	2.	Williams-Renault	18
5.	Riccardo Patrese (Italy)	9	3.	Ferrari	15
	Thierry Boutsen (Belgium)	9	4.	Tyrrell-Ford	14
7.	Nelson Piquet – Benetton Ford (Brazil)	6	5.	Benetton Ford	10
8.	Sandro Nannini – Benetton Ford (Italy)	4	6.	Arrows-Ford/Brabham-Judd	2
9.	Nigel Mansell (Great Britain)	3	8.	Larrousse-Lamborghini	1
10.	Stefano Modena (Italy)	2			
	Alex Caffi (Italy)	2			
12.	Eric Bernard (France)	1			
	Satoru Nakajima (Japan)	1			

Senna's win together with Berger's third place also put McLaren in a comfortable position in the Constructors' Championship:

It was doubtless no consolation whatsoever to Benetton that the man on top of the heap was a graduate from the Witney school of hard knocks during the Toleman days but at least Monaco was behind them – and it never did figure to be a Benetton triumph.

There was still room for hope with a large part of the season yet to come . . . and the major part of the decade . . .

Four Down and One Hundred and Fifty-Six to Come . . .

CHAPTER 10

Old Soldiers Never Die

Ayrton Senna, Alessandro Nannini, Nelson Piquet, Thierry Boutsen, Gerhard Berger, Riccardo Patrese, Michele Alboreto and Derek Warwick are members of the Toleman/ Benetton alumni, still very much alive and kicking in the Grand Prix firmament of the nineties.

Gerhard Berger, Benetton 'old boy' and now with McLaren.

Yet many other of 'the old boys' are still making news in their own way, some on the comeback trail, others in new careers, still more on the business side of motor racing.

Bruno Giacomelli (Toleman Class of '83) was placed four times in the top ten in fourteen starts with the Witney-based organisation and then retired from Grand Prix racing. Since then he has been engaged in other forms of racing and also with test driving for the Japanese-owned Leyton House Formula 1 team.

In the 1990 season he made his Grand Prix come-back. Another Japanese-owned team,

Life Racing, came new on the scene with Gary Brabham as their driver. As with many new teams, Life were off to a poor start and after the first two races of the season they approached Giacomelli to see if he would drive for them. The 37-year-old Italian had been around too long to imagine that he was being offered a passport to instant fame and fortune but he was stimulated enough by the challenge to ask Leyton House if they would release him. They readily did so with the stipulation that he continued to test for them.

Only time will tell if Giacomelli did the right thing. At the outset, he commented laconically, 'There is a great deal of work to be done.' The truth of that statement was underlined at Imola, venue of the 1990 San Marino Grand Prix. The car failed to complete a lap, the engine being damaged when an oil pump belt broke. And that was only in pre-qualifying – before the qualifying sessions and before the race itself. Someone unkindly commented that Bruno had been testing the wrong cars.

However, if anyone can get anything out of the Life car, life in fact, the veteran of sixty-nine Grands Prix races with Toleman, Alfa Romeo and McLaren is probably the man to do it.

Another 'old boy' on the sidelines at Imola was the Swedish ace, Stefan Johansson (Toleman Class of '84) but he was not behind a wheel for strictly legal reasons – legal in the literal sense.

Johansson had been contracted to the Onyx team which had changed ownership, being acquired by Swiss businessman Peter Monteverdi, who wanted to move the team's base of operations to that country. Johansson sought, and

James Hunt, British World Champion, now televison commentator.

obtained, an injunction to prevent this until the differences over his contract were sorted out. A sad thing to see a good driver on the sidelines.

Where do racing drivers go when they are sidelined for good? These days very often they go into television as commentators. Jackie Stewart has done it in the States and on British television. Another world champion, James Hunt, is also on British television as part of the regular Grand Prix commentating team with Murray Walker, while that fine Irish-born, Sussex-based driver, John Watson, is now a commentator for satellite television.

Pierluigi Martini (Toleman Class of '84) went one better.

After a narrow escape from death in the qualifiying stages of the San Marino Grand Prix – he had to be cut free – Pierluigi, injuries and all, returned on the Sunday (race-day) to commentate on the race for Italian television.

Preparing for life after racing?

One driver who quit Formula 1 to concentrate on business is Piercarlo Ghinzani (Toleman Class of '85). After ten years of Grand Prix racing the veteran Italian founded a company specialising in ecological cleaning products for cars, the community, industry and the building trade, with two brothers experienced in the field, Bruno and Mariucca Allegrini.

With the world becoming more and more ecology-minded, Piercarlo looked like being one of the first off the grid with products aimed at meeting the environmental demands of the nineties. His part in the operation is distribution and promotion, something he is no stranger to as his racing career has always run parallel with his business activities of selling cars. And although the new products are destined for a wide range of activities, the emphasis will still be on cleaning and cosmetic products for cars.

Nor do old soldiers really fade away.

Piercarlo hints that when the business is properly organised and he has established his sales network – an international one not just confined to Italy – then he might return to Group C racing. Convinced of the effectiveness

of racing cars as publicity vehicles, he also suggests that one of these days his sponsors will include A & G Chemical Car Service should he return to the race circuits.

Still very much part of the Grand Prix scene but also into business is Derek Warwick (Toleman Classes of '81, '82 and '83). He has gone into the classic car market, operating from his Jersey base. Warwick's company purchase cars for clients, offer an import and export service and provide storage and servicing facilities. Not any old cars you understand. We're talking Aston Martin, Ferrari, Lamborghini, Rolls-Royce and the like.

The big plus offered by Derek is his company's location in Jersey. The troublesome VAT does not apply there so all invoices are tax-free. Nor is that all. Car trading in Jersey is not subject to Capital Gains Tax which means it is possible for cars to be available at lower prices than would otherwise be the case. So now you can buy your classic car from one ex-Toleman driver and get another to clean it.

Another Toleman alumni could be involved in a new team. He is the man who headed the Toleman Grand Prix operation, Alex Hawkridge. If trackside talk is any guide, Alex is, in official language, 'assisting Reynard Racing Cars with their inquiries into Grand Prix racing.'

Reynard have made no secret of having Grand Prix ambitions but after their tremendous achievements in Formula 3 and Formula 3000 they have no intention of going in too soon and becoming just another of the courageous failures in the Formula 1 story.

A Formula 1 prototype was built in 1989, the car from Reynard's own design team, the engine a Mugen V8.With financial backing forthcoming – probably from Japan since no one else seems to have any these days – Reynard Cars might well make as big an impact in Formula 1 as they have done lower down the scale.

Should they do so an awful lot of people might get a quiet sense of satisfaction that from the ashes of the Toleman team have risen not one but two successful Grand Prix operations.

Appendix: How They Fared

Results in World Championship Grands Prix of Toleman and Benetton teams.
Compiled by Neil Eason Gibson.

1981

Toleman-Hart TG181
Drivers: No. 35 Brian Henton   No. 36 Derek Warwick

3. 5.81 **San Marino GP, Imola**
Did not qualify

17. 5.81 **Belgian GP, Zolder**
Did not qualify

31. 5.81 **Monaco GP**
Did not qualify

21. 6.81 **Spanish GP, Jarama**
Did not qualify

5. 7.81 **French GP, Dijon-Prenois**
Did not qualify

18. 7.81 **Marlboro British GP, Silverstone**
Did not qualify

2. 8.81 **German GP, Hockenheim**
Did not qualify

16. 8.81 **Austrian GP, Österreichring**
Did not qualify

30. 8.81 **Dutch GP, Zandvoort**
Did not qualify

13. 9.81 **Italian GP, Monza**
B. Henton   10th
D. Warwick   Did not qualify

27. 9.81 **Labatt Canadian GP, Montreal**
Did not qualify

17.10.81 **Caesars Palace GP, Las Vegas**
B. Henton   Did not qualify
D. Warwick   Retired 43 laps – gearbox –
                 when in 13th place

1982

Toleman-Hart TG183 (from Monza). Before TG181B and
  TG181C
Drivers: No. 35 Derek Warwick   No. 36 Teo Fabi

23. 1.82 **Quindrink-Pointerware South African GP,
         Kyalami**
D. Warwick   Retired 44 laps – accident
                 when in 19th place
T. Fabi   Did not qualify

21. 3.82 **Brazilian GP, Rio**
Did not qualify

4. 4.82 **Toyota GP of United States, Long Beach**
Did not qualify

25. 4.82 **San Marino GP, Imola** (FOCA boycott event)
D. Warwick   Retired 1 lap – electrics
T. Fabi   8 laps behind – not classified

9. 5.82 **Belgian GP, Zolder**
D. Warwick   Retired 29 laps – driveshaft
                 when 12th
T. Fabi   Retired 13 laps – brakes when
                 17th

23. 5.82 **Monaco GP**
Did not qualify

6. 6.82 **United States GP, Detroit**
Entries withdrawn

13. 6.82 **Labatt GP of Canada, Montreal**
Entries withdrawn

3. 7.82 **Dutch GP, Zandvoort**
D. Warwick   Retired 15 laps – engine spilt
                 oil
T. Fabi   Did not qualify

18. 7.82 **Marlboro British GP, Brands Hatch**
D. Warwick   Retired 41 laps – CV joint
              when 2nd
T. Fabi   Startline accident

25. 7.82 **French GP, Circuit Paul Ricard**
D. Warwick   15th
T. Fabi   Retired 1 lap – oil pump drive

8. 8.82 **German GP, Hockenheim**
D. Warwick   10th
T. Fabi   Did not qualify

15. 8.82 **Austrian GP, Österreichring**
D. Warwick   Retired 7 laps – rear suspension
              when 6th
T. Fabi   Retired 7 laps – drive shaft
              when 7th

29. 8.82 **Swiss GP, Dijon-Prenois**
D. Warwick   Retired 24 laps – engine when 23rd
T. Fabi   Retired 31 laps – misfire when
              12th

12. 9.82 **Italian GP, Monza**
D. Warwick   Retired 1 lap – spun off
T. Fabi   Retired 2 laps – engine cut out
              when 18th

25. 9.82 **Caesars Palace GP, Las Vegas**
D. Warwick   Retired 32 laps – misfire when
              16th
T. Fabi   Did not qualify

1983

Toleman-Hart TG183
Drivers: No. 35 Derek Warwick   No. 36 B.
               Giacomelli

13. 3.83 **Brazilian GP, Rio**
D. Warwick   8th
B. Giacomelli Spun off 16 laps when 19th

27. 3.83 **Toyota GP of United States, Long Beach**
D. Warwick   Retired 11 laps – tyre failure
              accident when 11th
B. Giacomelli Retired 26 laps – battery failure
              when 16th

17. 4. 83 **French GP, Circuit Paul Ricard**
D. Warwick   Retired 14 laps – engine/split
              water pipe when 14th
B. Giacomelli Retired 49 laps – gearbox
              when 11th

1. 5.83 **San Marino GP, Imola**
D. Warwick   Retired 27 laps – accident
B. Giacomelli Retired 21 laps – rear
              suspension

15. 5.83 **Monaco GP**
D. Warwick   Retired 50 laps – accident with
              Surer when 14th
B. Giacomelli Did not qualify

22. 5.83 **Belgian GP, Spa-Francorchamps**
D. Warwick   7th
B. Giacomelli 8th

5. 6.83 **United States GP, Detroit**
D. Warwick   Retired 25 laps – water leak
              when 7th
B. Giacomelli 9th

12. 6.83 **Labatt GP of Canada, Montreal**
D. Warwick   Retired 47 laps when 10th
B. Giacomelli Retired 43 laps when 11th

16. 7.83 **Marlboro British GP, Silverstone**
D. Warwick   Retired 27 laps – turbo charger
              when 9th
B. Giacomelli Retired 3 laps – gearbox when
              25th

7. 8.83 **German GP, Hockenheim**
D. Warwick   Retired 17 laps – engine when
              19th
B. Giacomelli Retired 19 laps – turbo when
              18th

14. 8.83 **Austrian GP, Österreichring**
D. Warwick   Retired 2 laps – turbo when
              24th
B. Giacomelli Retired 1 lap – accident
              damage when 25th

28. 8.83 **Dutch GP, Zandvoort**
D. Warwick   4th
B. Giacomelli Retired 68 laps when 13th

11. 9.83 **Italian GP, Monza**
D. Warwick   6th
B. Giacomelli 7th

25. 9.83 **John Player GP of Europe**
D. Warwick   5th
B. Giacomelli 6th

15.10.83 **Southern Sun Hotels GP, Kyalami**
D. Warwick   4th
B. Giacomelli Retired 56 laps – turbo fire
              when 12th

1983

Tyrell-Ford 012
Drivers: No. 3 Michele Alboreto   No. 4 Danny
Sullivan

13. 3.83	**Brazilian GP, Rio**	
	M. Alboreto	Retired 7 laps – incident with Baldi – damaged oil cooler
	D. Sullivan	11th
27. 3.83	**Toyota GP of United States, Long Beach**	
	M. Alboreto	9th
	D. Sullivan	8th
17. 4.83	**French GP, Circuit Paul Ricard**	
	M. Alboreto	8th
	D. Sullivan	Retired 21 laps – clutch
1. 5.83	**San Marino GP, Imola**	
	M. Alboreto	Retired 10 laps – accident
	D. Sullivan	Retired 37 laps – accident
15. 5.83	**Monaco GP**	
	M. Alboreto	Retired 0 laps – accident with Mansell
	D. Sullivan	5th
22. 5.83	**Belgian GP, Spa-Francorchamps**	
	M. Alboreto	14th
	D. Sullivan	12th
5. 6.83	**United States GP, Detroit**	
	M. Alboreto	1st
	D. Sullivan	Retired 30 laps – electrics
12. 6.83	**Labatt GP of Canada, Montreal**	
	M. Alboreto	8th equal
	D. Sullivan	8th equal
16. 7.83	**Marlboro British GP, Silverstone**	
	M. Alboreto	13th
	D. Sullivan	14th
7. 8.83	**German GP, Hockenheim**	
	M. Alboreto	Retired 4 laps – fuel pump drive
	D. Sullivan	12th
14. 8.83	**Austrian GP, Österreichring**	
	M. Alboreto	Retired 8 laps – accident
	D. Sullivan	Retired 0 laps – accident
28. 8.83	**Dutch GP, Zandvoort**	
	M. Alboreto	6th
	D. Sullivan	Retired 20 laps – engine failure

11. 9.83	**Italian GP, Monza**	
	M. Alboreto	Retired 29 laps – clutch
	D. Sullivan	Retired 44 laps – fuel pump drive
25. 9.83	**John Player GP of Europe**	
	M. Alboreto	Retired 65 laps – engine failure
	D. Sullivan	Retired 27 laps – fire/broken oil line
15.10.83	**Southern Sun Hotels GP, Kyalami**	
	M. Alboreto	Retired 60 laps – engine failure
	D. Sullivan	7th

1984

Toleman-Hart TG183B
Drivers: No. 19 A. Senna   No. 20 J. Cecotto

25. 3.84	**Brazilian GP, Rio**	
	A. Senna	Retired 8 laps – turbo boost pressure when 16th
	J. Cecotto	Retired 18 laps – turbo boost pressure when 20th
7. 4.84	**National Panasonic South African GP, Kyalami**	
	A. Senna	6th
	J. Cecotto	Retired 26 laps – tyre failure when 16th
29. 4.84	**Belgian GP, Zolder**	
	A. Senna	7th
	J. Cecotto	Retired 1 lap – clutch when 26th
6. 5.84	**San Marino GP, Imola**	
	A. Senna	Did not qualify
	J. Cecotto	8 laps behind – not classified
20. 5.84	**French GP, Dijon-Prenois**	
	A. Senna	Retired 35 laps – turbo when 10th
	J. Cecotto	Retired 22 laps – turbo when 17th
3. 6.84	**Monaco GP**	
	A. Senna	2nd
	J. Cecotto	Retired 1 lap – spun off when 14th
17. 6.84	**Labatt GP of Canada, Montreal**	
	A. Senna	7th
	J. Cecotto	9th

24. 6.84 **United States GP, Detroit**
A. Senna   Retired 21 laps – accident when 8th
J. Cecotto   Retired 23 laps – clutch when 15th

8. 7.84 **United States GP, Dallas**
A. Senna   Retired 47 laps – drive shaft when 13th
J. Cecotto   Retired 25 laps – hit wall when 16th

22. 7.84 **John Player Special British GP, Brands Hatch**
A. Senna   3rd
J. Cecotto   Did not start, practice accident

5. 8.84 **German GP, Hockenheim**
A. Senna   Retired 4 laps – rear wing failure when 5th
J. Cecotto   Not entered

19. 8.84 **Austrian GP, Österreichring**
A. Senna   Retired 35 laps – oil pressure when 4th
J. Cecotto   Not entered

26. 8.84 **Dutch GP, Zandvoort**
A. Senna   Retired 19 laps – engine when 9th

9. 9.84 **Italian GP, Monza**
S. Johansson   4th
A. Senna   Suspended by Toleman re contract
P. Martini   Did not qualify

7.10.84 **European GP, Nürburgring**
A. Senna   Retired 1 lap – accident
S. Johansson   Retired 17 laps – overheating when 12th

21.10.84 **Portuguese GP, Estoril**
A. Senna   3rd
A. Johansson   11th

1984

Benetton-Alfa Romeo 184T
Drivers: No. 22 Riccardo Patrese   No. 23 Eddie Cheever

25. 3.84 **Brazilian GP, Rio**
R. Patrese   Retired 41 laps – gearbox
E. Cheever   4th

7. 4.84 **National Panasonic South African GP, Kyalami**
R. Patrese   4th
E. Cheever   Retired 4 laps – damaged radiator

29. 4.84 **Belgian GP, Zolder**
R. Patrese   Retired 2 laps – ignition
E. Cheever   Retired 28 laps – engine

6. 5.84 **San Marino GP, Imola**
R. Patrese   Retired 6 laps – electrics
E. Cheever   8th – out of fuel

20. 5.84 **French GP, Dijon-Prenois**
R. Patrese   Retired 15 laps – engine
E. Cheever   Retired 51 laps – engine

3. 6.84 **Monaco GP**
R. Patrese   Retired 24 laps – steering
E. Cheever   Failed to qualify

17. 6.84 **Labatt GP of Canada, Montreal**
R. Patrese   Retired 37 laps – accident
E. Cheever   12th – out of fuel

24. 6.84 **United States GP, Detroit**
R. Patrese   Retired 20 laps – damaged suspension due to spin
E. Cheever   Retired 21 laps – engine

8. 7.84 **United States GP, Dallas**
R. Patrese   Retired 12 laps – hit wall
E. Cheever   Retired 8 laps – hit wall

22. 7.84 **John Player Special British GP, Brands Hatch**
R. Patrese   13th
E. Cheever   Retired 1 lap – accident damage

5. 8.84 **German GP, Hockenheim**
R. Patrese   Retired 16 laps – metering unit
E. Cheever   Retired 29 laps – engine

19. 8.84 **Austrian GP, Österreichring**
R. Patrese   10th – out of fuel
E. Cheever   Retired 18 laps – engine

26. 8.84 **Dutch GP, Zandvoort**
R. Patrese   Retired 51 laps – engine
E. Cheever   15th – out of fuel

9. 9.84 **Italian GP, Monza**
R. Patrese   3rd
E. Cheever   9th – out of fuel

7.10.84	**European GP, Nürburgring**	
	R. Patrese	6th
	E. Cheever	Retired 37 laps – fuel pump
21.10.84	**Portuguese GP, Estoril**	
	R. Patrese	8th
	E. Cheever	17th

1985

Toleman TG185
Drivers: No. 19 Teo Fabi   No. 20 Piercarlo Ghinzani

7. 4.85	**Brazilian GP, Rio**	
	Entries withdrawn	
21. 4.85	**Portuguese GP, Estoril**	
	Entries withdrawn	
5. 5.85	**San Marino GP, Imola**	
	Entries withdrawn	
19. 5.85	**Monaco GP**	
	T. Fabi	Retired 16 laps – turbo when placed 12th
16. 6.85	**Labatt GP of Canada, Montreal**	
	T. Fabi	Retired 3 laps – turbo when placed 24th
23. 6.85	**United States GP, Detroit**	
	T. Fabi	Retired 4 laps – clutch when placed 11th
7. 7.85	**French GP, Circuit Paul Ricard**	
	T. Fabi	Retired 49 laps – fuel pressure when placed 9th
21. 7.85	**Marlboro British GP, Silverstone**	
	T. Fabi	Retired 4 laps – crownwheel pinion when placed 9th
4. 8.85	**German GP, Nürburgring**	
	T. Fabi	Retired 29 laps – clutch when placed 8th
18. 8.85	**Austrian GP, Österreichring**	
	T. Fabi	Retired 31 laps – electrics when placed 15th
	P. Ghinzani	Engine failure during lap before race was stopped and restarted
25. 8.85	**Dutch GP, Zandvoort**	
	T. Fabi	Retired 18 laps – wheel bearing when placed 16th

	P. Ghinzani	Retired 12 laps – engine when placed 19th
8. 9.85	**Italian GP, Monza**	
	T. Fabi	12th
	P. Ghinzani	Stalled at start – retired
15. 9.85	**Belgian GP, Spa-Francorchamps**	
	T. Fabi	Retired 23 laps – throttle linkage when placed 12th
	P. Ghinzani	Retired 7 laps – accident when placed 14th
6.10.85	**Shell Oils GP of Europe, Brands Hatch**	
	T. Fabi	Retired 33 laps – engine when placed 14th
	P. Ghinzani	Retired 16 laps – engine when placed 14th
19.10.85	**Southern Sun Hotels GP, Kyalami**	
	T. Fabi	Retired 3 laps – engine when placed 9th
	P. Ghinzani	Retired 4 laps – engine when placed 15th
3.11.85	**Mitsubishi Australian GP, Adelaide**	
	T. Fabi	Retired 40 laps – engine when placed 12th
	P. Ghinzani	Retired 28 laps – clutch when placed 17th

1986

Benetton-BMW B186
Drivers: No. 19 Teo Fabi   No. 20 Gerhard Berger

27. 3.86	**Brazilian GP, Rio**	
	T. Fabi	10th
	G. Berger	6th
13. 4.86	**Tio Pepe GP of Spain, Jerez**	
	T. Fabi	5th
	G. Berger	6th
27. 4.86	**San Marino GP, Imola**	
	T. Fabi	Retired 39 laps – engine when placed 8th
	G. Berger	3rd
11. 5.86	**Monaco GP**	
	T. Fabi	Retired 17 laps – brakes when placed 19th
	G. Berger	Retired 42 laps – wheeldrive pegs when placed 6th

25. 5.86 **Belgian GP, Spa-Francorchamps**
    T. Fabi   7th
    G. Berger   10th

15. 6.86 **Labatt GP of Canada, Montreal**
    T. Fabi   Retired 13 laps – battery when placed 16th
    G. Berger   Retired 34 laps – turbo when placed 9th

22. 6.86 **United States GP, Detroit**
    T. Fabi   Retired 38 laps – gearbox when placed 13th
    G. Berger   Retired 8 laps – engine stopped when placed 9th

6. 7.86 **French GP, Circuit Paul Ricard**
    T. Fabi   Retired 7 laps – engine misfire when placed 18th
    G. Berger   Retired 22 laps – gearbox when placed 15th

13. 7.86 **Shell Oils British GP, Brands Hatch**
    T. Fabi   Retired 45 laps – fuel system when placed 6th
    G. Berger   Retired 22 laps – electrics when placed 3rd

27. 7.86 **German GP, Hockenheim**
    T. Fabi   Retired 1 lap – accident
    G. Berger   10th

10. 8.86 **Hungarian GP, Hungaroring**
    T. Fabi   Retired 32 laps – spun off/transmission when placed 11th
    G. Berger   Retired 44 laps – fuel leak/transmission when placed 5th

17. 8.86 **Austrian GP, Österreichring**
    T. Fabi   Retired 17 laps – engine when placed 6th
    G. Berger   7th

7. 9.86 **Italian GP, Monza**
    T. Fabi   Retired 44 laps – puncture when placed 11th
    G. Berger   5th

21. 9.86 **Portuguese GP, Estoril**
    T. Fabi   8th not running but classified
    G. Berger   Retired 44 laps – spun off incident with Johansson when placed 5th

12.10.86 **Mexican GP, Mexico**
    T. Fabi   Retired 4 laps – engine when placed 4th
    G. Berger   1st

26.10.86 **Foster's Australian GP, Adelaide**
    T. Fabi   10th
    G. Berger   Retired 40 laps – clutch engine when placed 11th

1987

Benetton B187 Ford-Cosworth Turbo
Drivers: No. 19 Teo Fabi   No. 20 Thierrry Boutsen

12. 4.87 **Brazilian GP, Rio**
    T. Fabi   Retired 9 laps – turbo when placed 4th
    T. Boutsen   5th

3. 5.87 **San Marino GP, Imola**
    T. Fabi   Retired 51 laps – turbo when placed 4th
    T. Boutsen   Retired 48 laps – engine when placed 5th

17. 5.87 **Belgian GP, Spa-Francorchamps**
    T. Fabi   Retired 34 laps – engine/oil pump drive when placed 4th
    T. Boutsen   Retired 18 laps – c/v joint when placed 11th

31. 5.87 **Monaco GP**
    T. Fabi   8th
    T. Boutsen   Retired 5 laps – c/v joint when placed 8th

21. 6.87 **United States GP, Detroit**
    T. Fabi   Retired 6 laps – accident with Cheever when placed 4th
    T. Boutsen   Retired 52 laps – brake disc when placed 7th

5. 7.87 **French GP, Circuit Paul Ricard**
    T. Fabi   5th
    T. Boutsen   Retired 31 laps – distributor drive when placed 4th

12. 7.87 **Shell Oils British GP, Silverstone**
    T. Fabi   6th
    T. Boutsen   7th

26. 7.87 **German GP, Hockenheim**
T. Fabi   Retired 18 laps – engine when
                placed 11th
T. Boutsen   Retired 26 laps – engine when
                placed 5th

9. 8.87 **Hungarian GP, Hungaroring**
T. Fabi   Retired 14 laps – gearbox when
                placed 12th
T. Boutsen   4th

16. 8.87 **Austrian GP, Österreichring**
T. Fabi   3rd
T. Boutsen   4th

6. 9.87 **Italian GP, Monza**
T. Fabi   7th
T. Boutsen   5th

20. 9.87 **Portuguese GP, Estoril**
T. Fabi   4th
T. Boutsen   14th

27. 9.87 **Tio Pepe Spanish GP, Jerez**
T. Fabi   Retired 40 laps – engine when
                placed 9th
T. Boutsen   Retired 66 laps – brakes/spun
                off when placed 3rd

18.10.87 **Mexican GP, Autodromo Hermanos
         Rodriguez**
T. Fabi   5th
T. Boutsen   Retired 15 laps – electronics
                when placed 2nd

1.11.87 **Fuji Television Japanese GP, Suzuka**
T. Fabi   Retired 16 laps – engine when
                placed 9th
T. Boutsen   5th

15.11.87 **Foster's Australian GP, Adelaide**
T. Fabi   Retired 46 laps – brakes when
                placed 14th
T. Boutsen   3rd

1988

Benetton B188 Ford V8
Drivers: No. 19 Alessandro Nannini
                No. 20 Thierry Boutsen

3. 4.88 **Brazilian GP, Rio**
A. Nannini   Retired 7 laps – engine
                overheating when placed 8th
T. Boutsen   7th

1. 5.88 **San Marino GP, Imola**
A. Nannini   6th
T. Boutsen   4th

15. 5.88 **Monaco GP**
A. Nannini   Retired 38 laps – gearbox when
                placed 5th
T. Boutsen   8th

29. 5.88 **Mexican GP, Autodromo Hermanos
         Rodriguez**
A. Nannini   7th
T. Boutsen   8th

17. 6.88 **Canadian GP, Montreal**
A. Nannini   Retired 15 laps – wastegate
                when placed 5th
T. Boutsen   3rd

19. 6.88 **United States GP, Detroit**
A. Nannini   Retired 14 laps – suspension
                damage when placed 4th
T. Boutsen   3rd

3. 7.88 **French GP, Circuit Paul Ricard**
A. Nannini   6th
T. Boutsen   Retired 28 laps – electrics when
                placed 24th

10. 7.88 **British GP, Silverstone**
A. Nannini   3rd
T. Boutsen   Retired 38 laps – c/v joint
                when placed 8th

24. 7.88 **German GP, Hockenheim**
A. Nannini   18th
T. Boutsen   6th

7. 8.88 **Hungarian GP, Hungaroring**
A. Nannini   Retired 24 laps – water leak
                when placed 8th
T. Boutsen   3rd

28. 8.88 **Belgian GP, Spa-Francorchamps**
A. Nannini   4th
T. Boutsen   3rd

11. 9.88 **Italian GP, Monza**
A. Nannini   9th
T. Boutsen   6th

25. 9.88 **Portuguese GP, Estoril**
A. Nannini   Retired 52 laps – driver
                exhausted due to vibration
                when placed 6th
T. Boutsen   3rd

2.10.88 **Spanish GP, Jerez**
A. Nannini   3rd
T. Boutsen   9th

30.10.88 **Japanese GP, Suzuka**
A. Nannini   5th
T. Boutsen   3rd

13.11.88 **Australian GP, Adelaide**
A. Nannini   Retired 63 laps – spun off when
                placed 11th
T. Boutsen   5th

1989

Benetton Ford B188 Ford DVR V8 then B189 then B189
Ford HB V8

Drivers: No. 19 Alessandro Nannini   No. 20 Johnny
                Herbert then Emmanuele Pirro

26. 3.89 **Brazilian GP, Autodromo Nelson Piquet**
A. Nannini   6th
J. Herbert   4th

23. 4.89 **San Marino GP, Imola**
A. Nannini   3rd
J. Herbert   11th

7. 5.89 **Monaco GP**
A. Nannini   8th
J. Herbert   14th

28. 5.89 **Mexican GP, Autodromo Hermanos
         Rodriquez**
A. Nannini   4th
J. Herbert   15th

4. 6.89 **United States GP, Phoenix**
A. Nannini   Retired 10 laps – driver fatigue
J. Herbert   5th

18. 6.89 **Molson GP of Canada, Circuit Gilles
         Villeneuve**
A. Nannini   Disqualified – illegal start from
                pitlane
J. Herbert   Did not qualify

9. 7.89 **Rhône-Poulenc GP of France, Circuit Paul
        Ricard**
A. Nannini   Retired 40 laps – suspension
                failure
E. Pirro   9th

16. 7.89 **British GP, Silverstone**
A. Nannini   3rd
E. Pirro   11th

30. 7.89 **German GP, Hockenheim**
A. Nannini   Retired 6 laps – ignition
E. Pirro   Retired 26 laps – accident

13. 8.89 **Hungarian GP, Hungaroring**
A. Nannini   Retired 46 laps – gear selector
E. Pirro   8th

27. 8.89 **Belgian GP, Spa-Francorchamps**
A. Nannini   5th
E. Pirro   10th

10. 9.89 **Italian GP, Monza**
A. Nannini   Retired 33 laps – brakes
E. Pirro   Retired 0 laps – gearbox

24. 9.89 **Portuguese GP, Estoril**
A. Nannini   4th
E. Pirro   Retired 29 laps – seized shock
                absorber

1.10.89 **Spanish GP, Jerez**
A. Nannini   Retired 14 laps – spun off
E. Pirro   Retired 59 laps – driver cramp

22.10.89 **Japanese GP, Suzuka**
A. Nannini   1st
E. Pirro   Retired 33 laps – accident

5.11.89 **Australian GP, Adelaide**
A. Nannini   2nd
E. Pirro   5th

Index

The Racers

Alboreto, Michele,　28, 54–7, 62, 93, 97, 102–4, 106, 107, 113, 119, 146,
　　151, 169, 177, 180
Alesi, Jean,　119, 146, 153, 156, 157, 162, 163, 166, 170, 171, 175, 176, 178, 179
Alliot, Philippe,　119, 144, 148, 151, 177
Amon, Chris,　46, 129
Andretti, Mario,　14, 76, 83, 105, 117, 153
Arnoux, Rene,　119, 148

Baldi, Mauro,　54
Barilla, Paolo,　148, 177, 178
Bell, Derek,　28
Berger, Gerhard,　17, 25, 27, 28, 42, 58, 62, 100, 107, 109, 115, 142, 144,
　　151, 153, 164, 166, 168–71, 177–80
Bernard, Eric,　148, 151, 177–9
Birkin, Sir Henry 'Tim',　139
Boutsen, Patricia,　112
Boutsen, Thierry,　18, 25, 28, 42, 46, 58, 70, 109, 110, 112, 115, 144, 151,
　　156, 157, 164, 166, 169, 171, 177–80
Brabham, David,　148, 168, 169, 176, 177
Brabham, Gary,　148, 151, 168, 180
Brabham, Geoff,　51, 148, 176
Brabham, Sir Jack,　46, 63, 85, 95, 119, 129, 148, 151
Breidenbach, Don,　51
Briggs, David,　51
Brundle, Martin,　18, 28, 57, 119, 123, 148

Caffi, Alex,　146, 169, 177–9
Capelli, Ivan,　115, 146, 177
Cecotto, Johnny,　39, 42, 97, 101, 107
Cevert, Francois,　38
Cheever, Eddie,　27, 28, 57, 95, 104, 105, 117, 119, 148, 168
Clark, Jimmy,　63, 67, 76, 123, 144

Dalmas, Yannick,　148
Daly, Derek,　50
Danner, Christian,　148
de Angelis, Elio,　51, 57, 68
de Cesaris, Andrea,　39, 119, 146, 156, 164, 170, 177
Dickson, Norman,　51
Donnelly, Martin,　144, 146, 151, 164, 171, 177
Dougall, Rad,　28, 50, 52, 72, 95
Duller, George,　28
Dumfries, Johnny,　22, 121, 148

Evans, Bob,　51

Fabi, Corrado,　100
Fabi, Teo,　28, 33, 35, 42, 46, 57, 58, 95, 99–101, 117
Fangio, Juan Manuel,　119, 121, 129
Fittipaldi, Emerson,　79, 163
Foitek, Gregor,　82, 148, 176–8

Gachon, Bertran,　148
Galicia, Divina,　51
Ganley, Howden,　38
Gethin, Peter,　38, 39
Ghinzani, Piercarlo,　42, 97, 99, 148, 182

Giacomelli, Bruno,　35, 36, 49, 95, 99, 180
Ginther, Richie,　7, 105
Giorgio, Carlo,　51
Gonzales, Froilan,　129
Grouillard, Olivier,　148, 151, 177
Gugelmin, Mauricio,　146, 177
Gurney, Dan,　105, 153

Hailwood, Mike,　38, 97
Hawthorn, Mike,　27, 144
Hayje, Boy,　51
Henton, Brian,　28, 31–3, 35, 48, 49, 51, 72, 93, 95, 96, 101
Herbert, Johnny,　20–5, 27, 28, 46, 58, 59, 103, 121, 123, 124, 126–8, 135,
　　144, 148, 151
Higgins, Derek,　48, 121, 126
Hill, Graham,　46, 65, 119, 144, 175
Hulme, Denny,　129
Hunt, James,　117, 177, 182

Ickx, Jackie,　109, 117

Johansson, Stefan,　27, 28, 42, 97, 101, 119, 146, 148, 180
Jones, Alan,　14, 117, 118
Jones, Stanley,　117

Larini, Nicola,　148, 151, 153, 177
Lauda, Niki,　57, 83, 109, 117–19
Lees, Geoff,　51, 100
Lehto, J.J.　148, 177

Mansell, Nigel,　17, 20, 25, 28, 62, 93, 102, 107, 115, 128, 144, 149, 151,
　　153, 157, 163, 164, 166, 168–70, 175, 176, 178, 179
Martini, Giancarlo,　100
Martini, Pierluigi,　100, 101, 148, 153, 169, 177, 182
McLaren, Bruce,　46, 129
McLaren, Iain,　51
McNish, Allan,　121
Merzario, Arturo,　102
Modena, Stefano,　148, 157, 159, 177, 179
Morbidelli, Giovanni,　151
Moreno, Roberto,　100, 148, 151, 177
Moss, Stirling,　144

Nakajima, Satoru,　138, 146, 151, 157, 162, 164, 177–9
Nannini, Alessandro,　16, 20, 22–5, 27, 28, 30, 46, 58, 59, 70, 85, 101, 107, 112,
　　113, 115, 121, 129, 135, 142, 151, 153, 162, 163, 166, 168–71, 176–80
Noble, Richard,　31
Nuvolari, Tazio,　97

Ongais, Danny,　76

Pace, Carlos,　119, 163
Palmer, Jonathan,　47, 119, 126, 148
Patrese, Riccardo,　28, 56, 57, 104, 105, 107, 112, 117, 144, 153, 164, 169–71, 177–80
Peterson, Ronnie,　38, 104
Piquet, Nelson,　22, 27, 28, 30, 80, 85, 96, 100, 102, 113, 115, 117–19, 121,
　　129, 135, 142, 151, 153, 156, 157, 160, 162–4, 166, 168–71, 176, 178–80
Pirro, Emmanuele,　20, 21, 25, 27, 28, 82, 112, 146, 151, 177
Prost, Alain,　16–18, 20, 27, 28, 35, 57, 93, 107, 112, 113, 115, 119, 123,
　　142, 144, 149, 151, 153, 156, 163, 164, 166, 169–71, 175, 176, 179

Raphanel, Pierre-Henri, 148
Regazzoni, Clay, 117, 123
Reutemann, Carlos, 119, 163
Riley, Brett, 51
Rindt, Jochen, 85, 119
Rosberg, Keke, 28, 38, 46, 57, 68
Rutherford, Johnny, 76

Sala, Luis Perez, 148
Scarfiotti, Lodovico, 102
Scheckter, Jody, 67
Schell, Harry, 104
Schneider, Bernd, 148
Senna, Ayrton, 16, 17, 18, 20, 28, 39, 42, 47, 91–3, 96, 97, 101, 102, 107, 109, 112, 115, 119, 126, 129, 135, 142, 144, 149, 151, 153, 156, 157, 160, 163, 164, 166, 168, 171, 175, 176, 178, 180
Sneva, Tom, 76
South, Stephen, 51
Sowery, Fred, 89
Stewart, Jackie, 46, 55, 78–80, 83, 93, 119, 123, 140, 144, 182
Sullivan, Danny, 54–6, 105, 106
Surer, Marc, 36, 96, 109
Surtees, John, 97
Suzuki, Aguri, 148, 151, 177

Tambay, Patrick, 14
Tarquini, Gabriele, 148
Taruffi, Piero, 97

Unser, Al, 76, 100

Warwick, Derek, 25, 28, 31–3, 35, 36, 38, 39, 48, 50, 93, 95–7, 101, 104, 112, 119, 135, 144–6, 164, 171, 177, 178, 180, 182
Watson, John, 102, 117, 119, 182
Weidler, Volker, 148
Winkelhock, Joachim, 148
Wollek, Bob, 110, 115

The Backroom Boys

Acquati, Lori, 48
Agnelli, Giannini, 142
Alexander, Tyler, 14
Ambrosie, Christine, 73
Ambrosie, Franco, 73
Ashcroft, Peter, 70

Balestre, Jean-Marie, 149, 168
Barnard, John, 17, 21, 28, 30, 60, 62, 135, 142, 150
Benetton, Alessandro, 28
Benetton, Carlo, 58
Benetton, Gilberto, 58
Benetton, Giulianna, 58
Benetton, Luciano, 28, 53, 58
Briatore, Flavio, 21, 26, 28, 60, 140, 142, 149
Broadley, Etic, 14
Bugatti, Ettore, 35
Byrne, Rory, 22, 26, 35, 52, 57, 71–4, 135, 142, 150, 171

Caliri, Giacomo, 113, 115
Chapman, Clive, 145
Chapman, Colin, 22, 46, 63, 65, 144, 145
Collins, Peter, 20, 21, 23, 25, 26, 46, 48, 57, 58, 74, 127
Cooper, John, 89
Copp, Harley, 67
Costin, Mike, 65, 75
Crooks, Paul, 73, 74

Delamont, Dean, 140
Dennis, Ron, 142, 153
Dernie, Frank, 144
Duckworth, Keith, 50, 63, 65, 68, 74–6

Earle, Mike, 97
Ecclestone, Bernie, 85, 100, 118, 140, 149, 168

Ferrari, Enzo, 102
Ferris, Geoffrey, 130
Forghieri, Mauro, 144
Francis, Alf, 87, 88
Fry, Pat, 74, 88

Gentry, John, 35, 74
Gillen, Stanley, 67
Goddard, Geoff, 75, 76

Haas, Carl, 14
Hart, Brian, 14, 31, 50–2, 95
Hawkridge, Alex, 57, 93, 182
Hayes, Walter, 67
Head, Patrick, 144

Jones, Parnelli, 76
Jordan, Eddie, 28, 126, 146

Kranefuss, Michael, 21, 63, 68–71, 135, 137, 162

Lewis, Peter, 87, 88
Ligier, Guy, 67
Lini, Franco, 168

Mathie, Tony, 127, 128
Mayer, Teddy, 14
McCormack, Mark, 140
Mehl, Leo, 80
Message, Gordon, 21, 25, 27, 48, 74, 135, 149–51, 162, 168, 169
Minardi, Giancarlo, 113, 115
Monteverdi, Peter, 180
Murray, Gordon, 119

Newman, Paul, 14
Nichol, Don, 73
Nichols, Steve, 142, 144
Nunn, Mo, 118

Oliver, Jackie, 73, 96, 103

Paget, Hon. Dorothy, 139
Penske, Roger, 129
Pilette, Andre, 109
Postlethwaite, Harvey, 176
Purdy, John, 77

Rees, Alan, 73
Riccono, Charles, 168
Russell, Jim, 106
Russell, Richard, 150

Scammell, Dick, 75, 76, 150, 162, 168, 174
Schenken, Tim, 18
Silman, Roger, 134, 149
Southgate, Tony, 73
Stepney, Nigel, 27, 74, 134
Symonds, Pat, 74

Tauranac, Ron, 95
Toleman, Ted, 31, 93
Tyrrell, Ken, 54, 55, 176

Vogt, Christian, 149

Walker, Murray, 182
Walters, Martin, 75, 76
Wass, Dave, 73, 74
Weslake, Harry, 50
Wheatcroft, Tom, 76
Williams, Frank, 146
Witty, Chris, 52

Young, Eoin, 48, 88